CRITICAL ESSAYS ON

RICHARD II

William Shakespeare

Editors:
Linda Cookson
Bryan Loughrey

LONGMAN
LITERATURE
GUIDES

Longman Literature Guides

Editors: Linda Cookson and Bryan Loughrey

Titles in the series:

CONTENTS

PREFACE

Like all professional groups, literary critics have developed their own specialised language. This is not necessarily a bad thing. Sometimes complex concepts can only be described in a terminology far removed from everyday speech. Academic jargon, however, creates an unnecessary barrier between the critic and the intelligent but less practised reader.

This danger is particularly acute where scholarly books and articles are re-packaged for a student audience. Critical anthologies, for example, often contain extracts from longer studies originally written for specialists. Deprived of their original context, these passages can puzzle and at times mislead. The essays in this volume, however, are all specially commissioned, self-contained works, written with the needs of students firmly in mind.

This is not to say that the contributors — all experienced critics and teachers — have in any way attempted to simplify the complexity of the issues with which they deal. On the contrary, they explore the central problems of the text from a variety of critical perspectives, reaching conclusions which are challenging and at times mutually contradictory.

They try, however, to present their arguments in direct, accessible language and to work within the limitations of scope and length which students inevitably face. For this reason, essays are generally rather briefer than is the practice; they address quite specific topics; and, in line with examination requirements, they incorporate precise textual detail into the body of the discussion.

They offer, therefore, working examples of the kind of essay-writing skills which students themselves are expected to develop. Their diversity, however, should act as a reminder that in the field of literary studies there is no such thing as a 'model' answer. Good essays are the outcome of a creative engagement with literature, of sensitive, attentive reading and careful thought. We hope that those contained in this volume will encourage students to return to the most important starting point of all, the text itself, with renewed excitement and the determination to explore more fully their own critical responses.

How to use this volume

Obviously enough, you should start by reading the text in question. The one assumption that all the contributors make is that you are already familiar with this. It would be helpful, of course, to have read further — perhaps other works by the same author or by influential contemporaries. But we don't assume that you have yet had the opportunity to do this and any references to historical background or to other works of literature are explained.

You should, perhaps, have a few things to hand. It is always a good idea to keep a copy of the text nearby when reading critical studies. You will almost certainly want to consult it when checking the context of quotations or pausing to consider the validity of the critic's interpretation. You should also try to have access to a good dictionary, and ideally a copy of a dictionary of literary terms as well. The contributors have tried to avoid jargon and to express themselves clearly and directly. But inevitably there will be occasional words or phrases with which you are unfamiliar. Finally, we would encourage you to make notes, summarising not just the argument of each essay but also your own responses to what you have read. So keep a pencil and notebook at the ready.

Suitably equipped, the best thing to do is simply begin with whichever topic most interests you. We have deliberately organised each volume so that the essays may be read in any order. One consequence of this is that, for the sake of clarity and self-containment, there is occasionally a degree of overlap between essays. But at least you are not forced to follow one — fairly arbitrary — reading sequence.

Each essay is followed by brief 'Afterthoughts', designed to highlight points of critical interest. But remember, these are only there to remind you that it is *your* responsibility to question what you read. The essays printed here are not a series of 'model' answers to be slavishly imitated and in no way should they be regarded as anything other than a guide or stimulus for your own thinking. We hope for a critically involved response: 'That was interesting. But if *I* were tackling the topic . . .!'

Read the essays in this spirit and you'll pick up many of the skills of critical composition in the process. We have, however, tried to provide more explicit advice in 'A practical guide to essay writing'. You may find this helpful, but do not imagine it offers any magic formulas. The quality of your essays ultimately depends on the quality of your engagement with literary texts. We hope this volume spurs you on to read these with greater understanding and to explore your responses in greater depth.

A note on the text

All references are to the New Penguin Shakespeare edition of *Richard II*, ed. Stanley Wells.

Andrew Gibson

Andrew Gibson is a Lecturer in English at the University of London and writes both fiction and criticism. His latest academic publication is Reading Narrative Discourse: Studies in the Novel from Cervantes to Beckett.

ESSAY

Richard II: the misfit as hero

Richard II has often been regarded as a poetic figure, adrift in a philistine, political world. Those particularly responsible for this view were Walter Pater and the poet William Butler Yeats. Yeats thought that, when they were looking at the history plays, too many critics believed that Shakespeare's criterion was 'efficiency in action'. These critics felt that Shakespeare sided with his more energetically and aggressively competent kings, the men of the world, like Henry V. They assumed that Shakespeare was critical of the other type of king — like Richard II, who was supposedly 'sentimental', 'weak', 'selfish' and 'insincere'. Yeats argued that such critics delighted 'in abasing Richard II'. Theirs was the delight schoolboys get out of 'persecuting some boy of fine temperament, who has weak muscles and a distaste for school games'. But Yeats himself did not imagine 'that Shakespeare preferred the men who deposed Richard' to Richard himself. That, he said, would be to suppose 'that Shakespeare judged men with the eyes of a Municipal Councillor weighing the merits of a Town Clerk'. Richard, Yeats argued, is a 'wild creature'. He possesses a contemplative temperament, and a gift of 'lyrical phantasy'. The trouble is that he's a 'vessel of porcelain'. He's therefore likely to come to grief in a world too harsh for him. It's the harshness of the world, however, that's to blame for that.[1]

Of course, this is a rather precious idea. It's indulgent, and that may possibly make us feel rather nastier about 'vessels of porcelain' than we would otherwise feel. But, in any case, Yeats surely can't convince us that Richard is primarily a sensitive plant, at odds with a world of brutes. Yeats's case rests on a view of Richard as 'lovable'. But in some ways it's very hard to like Richard at all. We can quickly come up with a list of complaints about the early Richard, for instance. He is pathetically unable to control the progress of the quarrel between Bolingbroke and Mowbray, and tries to mask his failure behind a sort of bogus authoritarianism (I.1.196–200). When he tries to make sure that Bolingbroke and Mowbray do not 'Embrace each other's love in banishment,' he just looks politically hapless (I.3.178–190). We have the same impression when he abruptly confiscates Bolingbroke's goods and lands (II.1.210). But these deficiencies are due to mistakes in calculation, or shortage of clout. They might merely seem to support Yeats's point. The early Richard's arrogance and superciliousness tell rather more heavily against him. When (ironically) he tells Mowbray, for instance, that it 'boots him not' to be 'compassionate' (self-pitying) Richard comes across as false, vainglorious and slightly petulant. (I.3.174). Similarly, he can be contemptuous about ordinary folk. That's evident in his reference to the 'slaves' on whom Bolingbroke supposedly 'throws away' reverence (I.4.27). His attitudes to the Irish, too, are those of the brutal, confident coloniser (II.1.156–158). But it's Gaunt, and Richard's treatment of Gaunt, that make Richard look worst. Gaunt provides a powerful indictment of Richard as having failed, through vanity and indifference, to protect the English Eden (II.1.31–68). And Richard's responses to the dying Gaunt undoubtedly show his shabbiest side: trivial, hard-hearted, incapable of any adequately human response to ordinary mortality (I.4.59–64; II.1.69–138). It's not surprising to find Shakespeare clearly directing irony at the early Richard. He makes Richard refer,

---

[1] W B Yeats, 'At Stratford-upon-Avon', in *Ideas of Good and Evil* (Dublin, 1905), pp. 142–168, *passim*.

for example, to the 'unstooping firmness' of his own 'upright soul' (I.1.121). This is not a self-image — to say the very least — that Richard and the play will sustain.

One might argue, of course, that all this isn't very important, because Richard leaves this shallow self behind. He becomes a sadder figure, and a deeper one. But the later Richard is often hard to warm to as well. He is melodramatic, for example, as in his repeated attempts to cast himself as a suffering Christ-figure (III.2.130–132; IV.1.170, 241). Those not sympathetic to him continually point out how self-dramatising he can be. Act III, scene 2, for example, shows Richard passing through a series of self-dramatising responses to his plight. Circumstances turn successive ironies on those responses. That is very much the effect of Shakespeare's cunning arrangement of the scene. Suddenly events hugely outstrip Richard's power to cope with them. He responds by posturing. He hasn't had time to grow into any properly adult seriousness, and the postures are embarrassing and poignant substitutes for it. Richard is also given to futile outbursts. Apart from anything else, they suggest that his contact with reality is rather frail. This is the case in III.3, for example, when Richard suddenly suggests to Aumerle that they 'send/ Defiance to the traitor, and so die' (III.3.129–130). The frailty of the contact is characteristic of Richard for more or less the whole of the play. It is usually faintly alienating. It's likely to put us off Richard's incredulity, for instance, as he looks in his 'glass' and finds his deposition has left 'No deeper wrinkles' (IV.1.277). It also puts us off his over-fine farewell to his queen (V.1.86–102). Richard frequently seems reluctant to face realities, including the reality of his own grief. It's his queen who actually offers one of the most telling criticisms of him. Unlike the deposed Richard, she says, even in its hopeless situation, 'The lion dying thrusteth forth his paw/ And wounds the earth, if nothing else, with rage/ To be o'erpowered' (V.1.29–31). Where is the truth of Richard's most fundamental and passionate response to his plight? The answer is that, right the way through to the end of the play, he's evading it. That's why he's tempted to find himself a 'traitor with the rest' (IV.1.247).

So Richard's evasiveness is unattractive, irresponsible, less than fully human — and yet . . . . In describing him that way, we're starting to sound like Yeats's Municipal Councillor (or a pompous headteacher. A surprising number of literary critics do sometimes sound like that). In Richard's case, it won't quite work. Such judgements aren't exactly wrong, or irrelevant to the play. They just don't quite seem to come from the most fitting point of view. Some of Shakespeare's greatest heroes and heroines aren't very responsible, or even 'fully human'. They aren't very likeable either. For that matter, some of the most compelling figures in literature are often not very likeable. In Homer's *Iliad*, for instance, Achilles spends the greater part of the poem sulking in his tent. To Homer, however, it doesn't matter all that much. It's what and how much Achilles is capable of *doing* that matters. In Shakespeare's plays the emphasis is similar, but also different. In the case of Hamlet, Lear or Richard it's what and how much they are capable of thinking, feeling and *being* that matters. Yeats and his fellow-enthusiasts certainly did over-value Richard's alleged unworldliness and exquisite sensitivity. But they were surely right to feel that Richard was far closer to Shakespeare than Bolingbroke could conceivably be. Apart from anything else, as Walter Raleigh remarked in 1909, it is difficult to condemn Richard without taking sides against poetry.

Richard, then, isn't likeable. On the other hand, he is subtle, complicated and fascinating. Complexity of that order has its own virtues. They may compensate for a certain lack of amiability. As in the case of Hamlet or Lear, what's important is that Richard is somehow beyond or apart from us. In the first instance, of course, that's a question of rank. But it's ultimately also a question of the whole personality. Richard is a very curious hybrid. Shakespeare's main source for the play, Holinshed, stressed Richard's indulgence in what he calls 'the filthie sinne of leacherie and fornication'. Shakespeare makes little of this. But his Richard is nonetheless a sensualist, whilst also an intellectual. Richard is a king without kingliness. He is poetically inventive, but not a poet. In the early stages of the play, he is an intermittent plotter without any real scheme. He is sometimes politically feckless, as we've seen. But he can also be astute, as when he cuts through York's rhetorical protestation of Gaunt's 'love' for him (II.1.145–146). Richard is capable of high philosophy. But he is also capable — almost simultaneously — of arrant childishness. In III.2, for example, he swings, within 30 lines, from a dignified assertion of common humanity to a plaintive notion of 'pining away' in Flint Castle (III.2.175–210). Sometimes he is lofty and full of hauteur. At other times he is self-deprecating and self-abasing, letting his 'wretchedness' bait 'himself' (IV.1.237). The paradox, here, is nicely caught in Richard's very lordly protest that he no longer has any lordly power over Northumberland (IV.1.253).

In part, Richard's contradictions are the result of the abrupt changes in his circumstances. But much about him also suggests a psychologically determined instability of character existing long before his loss of the throne. At the very beginning of the play, we find Richard posing as the responsible, judicious monarch arbitrating between tempestuous lords, or 'ruling' the 'wrath-kindled gentlemen', as he puts it (I.1.152). But the pose is soon demolished by his impulsive behaviour at Coventry (I.3.119–120). The erratic quality of that behaviour is emphasised by the contrast between it and the formality preceding it in the scene. The emphasis seems appropriate. For everything else that we see of Richard effectively unfolds from this first, decisive moment of caprice. Indeed, so does the action of the whole play. The Richard who emerges is, above all, *volatile*. Even his treatment of the dying Gaunt gives proof of volatility. Earlier in the play, Richard has actually treated Gaunt respectfully, and even affectionately, as when he tries to get Gaunt to calm Bolingbroke (I.1.159). But that Richard should switch abruptly from one emotional attitude to Gaunt to a very different one is not surprising. He keeps on changing like this throughout the play. Again and again, his reactions are spontaneous, triggered off by immediate stimuli, inconsistent with one another. Thus, when Gaunt takes him to task for his conduct, Richard calls him 'a lunatic lean-witted fool' (II.1.115). But, when York reprimands him and warns him, Richard makes him Lord Governor of England (II.1.186–220). Similarly, Richard has only to see Gaunt's 'grieved heart' in the 'glasses' of his eyes to 'pluck' four years off the period of Bolingbroke's banishment. (I.3.208–211). On his return from Ireland, he makes a long, rhetorical address to English soil. Then he promptly dismisses his own words as 'senseless conjuration' (III.2.6–23). In III.2, the King confident of divine aid at lines

60–62 has virtually surrendered by lines 80–81. Richard can be wholly overcome by an 'ague-fit of fear' and then shrug it off again, almost at once (III.2.144–190). In III.3, he seems to accept the fact that he must exchange his 'large kingdom for a little grave' (III.3.154). Then he turns out to be quite obviously reluctant to do so. It's hard for him to recognise that 'like glistering Phaethon,/ Wanting the manage of unruly jades,' he really must 'come down' (III.3.178–179). It's therefore hardly surprising, at the climactic point, when Bolingbroke asks Richard whether he is 'contented to resign the crown', to find Richard beginning his reply in hesitant and contradictory terms:

Ay, no. No, ay; for I must nothing be.

(IV.1.200)

The seesaw quality of the line matches the seesawing game with the crown immediately preceding it.

But perhaps the most interesting moment of this kind occurs at the end of the play, just before Richard is murdered. In the earlier part of V.5, Richard seems to be moving towards philosophical resignation to his lot. The sequence with the groom confirms this. Richard is apparently starting to recognise his kinship with ordinary humanity (V.5.67–94). But then the keeper comes in with the food. He refuses to taste it, and Richard strikes him:

The devil take Henry of Lancaster, and thee!
Patience is stale, and I am weary of it.

(V.5.102–103)

This might seem an extraordinary outburst. Actually, the detail is there in Holinshed. In Holinshed, however, it's consistent with the previous Richard. In Shakespeare's play, the reverse is the case. So any pretence of Richard's to philosophy fades and vanishes. Another mood and attitude overtake him. Then the new impatience itself yields to a fresh burst of whimsicality. The murderers rush in and find Richard wondering what death might 'mean' by assaulting him so 'rudely' (V.5.105). Shakespeare doesn't allow Richard the (rather banal) luxury of a fine philosophical conclusion. He keeps him faithful to himself to the end, which means constant in his liability to change.

The adjective most appropriate to Richard is probably 'unstaid'. It's a word that Gaunt uses of him early in the play (II.1.2). In Shakespeare's day, it had several meanings. It could mean 'not staid', not regulated or orderly in one's conduct. It could also mean 'not *stayed*' — without a 'stay' — and thus be used of someone who hadn't been restrained or controlled; someone likely to change, not stable or settled in their opinions or resolves. Of course, Richard hasn't had much restraint imposed on him. That's clear from what York has to say about him having every new vanity 'buzzed into his ears' as soon as it has been 'thrust forth' (II.1.24–26). Apart from that, Richard is obviously 'unstaid' in the other senses of the word. That's obvious enough from what I've said so far.

It's certainly possible to interpret Richard's volatility in a negative light. Critics have sometimes seen a 'lurking hysteria' in him, for instance, and it's not hard to see what they're implying.[2] Bolingbroke is a good, solid male, and therefore a kingly sort of fellow. Richard is hysterical and womanish, and therefore a bad king and a 'monarchiser'. But actually Richard's 'womanish instability' is partly evidence of a kind of richness, an indication of uniqueness. For Richard is many-selved, or — to use a word that the poet Coleridge used of Shakespeare himself — 'myriad-minded'.[3] Richard really is gifted with something like the artistic temperament. But that's got nothing to do with any ethereal otherworldliness, which is what Yeats seemed to think. What's important is that Richard partly shares his creator's multiplicity of mind, his lack of congealed self. The difference, of course, is that Richard is not a poet or dramatist. All the same, the point helps us to understand the significance of Richard's long soliloquy at the beginning of V.5. In prison, solitude, stillness and uncertainty make him much more aware of what he really is (and is not). He expresses it all in a speculative kind of thinking, of course. But a new sense of himself is nonetheless clearly dawning:

---

[2] See, for instance, A R Humphreys, *Shakespeare: Richard II* (London, 1967), p. 55.

[3] S T Coleridge, *Biographia Literaria* (London, 1975), p. 175.

> My brain I'll prove the female to my soul,
> My soul the father, and these two beget
> A generation of still-breeding thoughts,
> And the same thoughts people this little world,
> In humours like the people of this world.
>
> (V.5.6–10)

It's worth remembering that the person talking here is still youthful. An actor could conceivably deliver these lines in a tone of real excitement — the excitement of a young man who recognises for the first time that the qualities that have stopped him functioning effectively in the outside world are also *enqbling*. Certainly, the lines suggest that a kind of creative power is awakening in Richard, even if it can't be separated from deep discontent. Throughout the play, we've been made aware of how varied Richard's thoughts and feelings are, how relative his decisions and resolutions, how alterable his definitions and versions of himself. Now, in V.5, his attitude towards his own 'variety' becomes much more playful:

> Sometimes am I king,
> Then treasons make me wish myself a beggar;
> And so I am. Then crushing penury
> Persuades me I was better when a king.
> Then am I kinged again; and by and by
> Think that I am unkinged by Bolingbroke,
> And straight am nothing.
>
> (V.5.32–38)

Richard's self-cancellations have continually left him on the brink of 'nothing'. But if he's innocent of any identity, he can't be content with nothingness either. He finally sees that for himself:

> But whate'er I be,
> Nor I, nor any man that but man is,
> With nothing shall be pleased . . .
>
> (V.5.38–40)

The alternative for Richard, however, has been playing 'in one person many people' (V.5.31). Prison means that he stops playing 'many people' in the outside world. Instead, he starts 'breeding' them inside his head. Richard's real tragedy is that he is murdered just as he has become vitally conscious of his own imaginative resources.

Earlier in the play, those resources express themselves in irony, wit, ingenious or whimsical speculation. Once again, they're connected to Richard's dividedness. Irony is a way of negotiating the claims of different commitments. The ironist simultaneously expresses different and even opposed feelings and attitudes. Richard uses irony a lot, particularly after his return from Ireland. Take, for example, his well-known assertion of divine right:

> Not all the water in the rough rude sea
> Can wash the balm off an anointed king.
> The breath of worldly men cannot depose
> The deputy elected by the Lord.
> For every man that Bolingbroke hath pressed
> To lift shrewd steel against our golden crown,
> God for his Richard hath in heavenly pay
> A glorious angel.

> (III.2.54–61)

Can Richard really be serious here? The answer, of course, is 'ay, no'. He's more serious at the beginning of the passage than the end. As he proceeds, he seems to become more aware that what he's saying isn't really convincing, may even be ludicrous. Part of him very much wants to believe in his divine right to the throne. Part of him actually does believe in it. And part of him is inclined to scoff at the whole idea. Once again, different selves are warring within him. The irony keeps them all in play. The speculative side to his mind also allows him to say things that part of him means, and another part does not. Richard's image of the well and buckets, for instance, is partly a way of expressing his grief, partly a way of holding it at a distance. But it also surreptitiously conveys something fiercer: a contempt for the shallower Bolingbroke as the 'emptier' bucket 'dancing in the air' (IV.1.180–188). Similarly, Richard's threat of God's vengeance in III.3 is ambiguous in tone:

> Yet know, my master, God omnipotent,
> Is mustering in his clouds on our behalf,
> Armies of pestilence, and they shall strike
> Your children yet unborn and unbegot,

> That lift your vassal hands against my head
> And threat the glory of my precious crown.
>
> (III.3.85–90)

On a literal level, this is a childish fantasy, and Richard knows it (though he would also like the fantasy to come true). On a metaphorical level, however, it's a shrewd and dignified forecast of the havoc likely to result from Bolingbroke's usurpation. Again, Richard is being several things at once. He can be several things at once, however, only because Shakespeare gives him an intricate mind, and a marvellous command of language. In this sense, Raleigh was right. But to take sides against Richard is to take sides, in particular, against the *richness of response* that Shakespeare's finest poetry expresses.

Richness of response is not characteristic \of the other figures in *Richard II*. By and large, the play gives us a world of direct talk and direct action. In this world, the only alternative to directness is usually flattery and deceit. Like Hamlet in Claudius's rotten Denmark, Richard inevitably looks out of place in such a world. In other words, he's bound to be a misfit. He's too complex to fit easily into any of the roles he is called on to play. He can't quite be either the ruler as arbitrator, or the lawful king wrongfully deposed, or the humble yielder, the grief-filled husband or the philosophical loser. Whenever he tries to throw himself into such roles, another side of him starts to come out as well. The result is that he's always rather detached from his roles. Critics have often thought of Richard as basically an actor. But it's Bolingbroke who's the *good* actor, identified with his part. York brings this home to us in the description of the two men's coming into London. It was Bolingbroke, says York, who was the 'well graced actor'. Richard was more like 'him that enters next', whose 'prattle' is likely to be thought 'tedious' (V.2.23–28). Richard's predicament lies, not in his being an actor, but in his never quite being at one with any of his roles. He thus keeps reminding us of the fact that he is an actor. In a fiercely political world, it's a disastrous flaw. It's likely only to amaze others, or alienate them.

Some of the best comment that we have on Shakespeare comes in the letters of the poet John Keats. In a letter to his brothers, George and Thomas, Keats once described a quality he thought was crucial to 'Achievement in literature'. He called it *'Negative Capability,* that is when a man is capable of being in uncertainties, Mysteries, doubts, without any irritable reaching after fact & reason.'[4] He suggested that Shakespeare possessed an enormous amount of 'Negative Capability'. In other words, Shakespeare was a genius partly because he could think, feel and be more than one thing at once. He was the finest example of what Keats elsewhere called 'the camelion Poet', fully endowed with 'the poetical Character'. Keats thought that the poetical character had 'no self'. It is 'every thing and nothing', he wrote. It 'enjoys light and shade; it lives in gusto, be it foul or fair, high or low, rich or poor, mean or elevated ... A Poet is the most unpoetical of any thing in existence; because he has no Identity.' Keats goes on to add of himself that (presumably because he's a poet) 'not one word I ever utter can be taken for granted as an opinion growing out of my identical nature — how can it, when I have no nature?'[5] Richard could very well have said the same. Much of what Keats says of Shakespeare could also be said of Richard. But Richard is the 'camelion' without the poetry. He's therefore fated to be a misfit in a world to which he's unsuited. Thinking of Richard, Yeats remarked that men 'are made useless to the State as often by abundance as by emptiness'. It's an inner 'abundance' that finally makes Richard a tragic figure.

---

[4] John Keats, letter to George and Thomas Keats, 22 December 1817, in *Letters,* edited by M B Forman (London, 1952), p. 71.
[5] Keats, letter to Richard Woodhouse, 27 October 1818, in *Letters,* pp. 226–227.

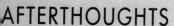

AFTERTHOUGHTS

1

In what ways does Richard attempt to 'cast himself as a suffering Christ-figure' (page 11)?

2

'Richard, then, isn't likeable' (page 12): has Gibson proved his case?

3

What can you learn by a comparison of Shakespeare's character Richard II with the Richard in the source material?

4

Explain the relevance to the argument of this essay of the description in its final paragraph of 'Negative Capability'.

Nicholas Potter

Nicholas Potter is Senior Lecturer in English at the West Glamorgan Institute of Higher Education. He has published on Shakespeare in Shakespeare: the Play of History *(Macmillan, 1987) by Graham Holderness, Nicholas Potter and John Turner.*

ESSAY

'This sceptred isle': the idea of England in *Richard II*

What does John of Gaunt mean by 'sceptred' in his famous speech, learned by heart by generations of school students undergoing their training into the national heritage? I ask the question in this deliberately, even gratuitously, provocative manner because I think that *Richard II* is concerned with the national heritage, and I do not think that the question is historical or merely abstract. After all, we live in a nation-state called (evocatively if imprecisely) 'Britain': we are sometimes referred to by politicians and other zealously patriotic public figures (such as newsreaders and sports commentators) as 'Britons'; we write ourselves on our passports and other official documents (such as college application forms) as 'British'.

We are considering the language of definition and self-definition which hovers incessantly and often unsatisfactorily about the groupings we want to claim to belong to or to which we are assigned. More particularly, we are considering what is taken to be the defining characteristic of these groupings. Our 'country' is, or claims to be, the coincidence of 'national' and political boundaries, expressed in such symbols as the flag, and such institutions as the monarchy. In international diplomatic circles (and for the Eurovision Song Contest) we are known as the United Kingdom.

The flag, the Union Jack, records a union that lasted just over 120 years. In 1801 Ireland was declared to be united with England, Scotland and Wales. England had been united with Wales since 1536, and with Scotland since 1707 (though England and Scotland had had joint sovereigns since 1601). Ireland seceded from this union in 1922, leaving a United Kingdom of Great Britain and Northern Ireland. The 'country' John of Gaunt is talking about is strictly 'England', more strictly than it was when Shakespeare wrote *Richard II*, because it was by that time, England and Wales. It is not pedantry to point out that John of Gaunt was born in Ghent, which was (and is) in what is now called Belgium.

'Britain' (first used in 1604, when James I was proclaimed 'King of Great Britain', that is, England, Wales and Scotland, known at that time respectively as 'Britannia prima', 'Britannia secunda' and 'North Britain') is a name for the country first bestowed by its Roman rulers, who called its inhabitants 'Britones', perhaps after the name given to itself by one of the Celtic tribes. The Celts themselves were not aboriginal inhabitants, but were themselves invaders. The Angles and the Saxons (the first of whom gave the name 'Aenglish' to what became the language we speak) came in the wake of the Romans' departure, followed by the Vikings sporadically, and, in 1066, by the Normans (who were Vikings who had settled in Northern France), who established the line which, not without the occasional hiccup, leads to Richard II. The English kings were traced by Geoffrey of Monmouth in his *Historia Regum Britanniae* (1136) to Brutus, great-grandson of Aeneas, the hero of Virgil's epic poem, *Aeneid*. The language, which Mowbray declares he loves, only became the language of England officially when in 1362 it was established as the language to be used in the courts. The language Mowbray would have spoken was not the language he speaks in the play and which he declares he loves. This is important because the language is taken by the play to be a defining feature of the nation and of the country, and, as the foregoing sketch of its history suggests, it is not all that easily defined, except perhaps with the assistance of legend, as in Geoffrey of Monmouth's case.

Language in the play has a pervasive tone which emerges the more strongly at moments such as Mowbray's departure into exile, but which characterises the play as a whole. It is a note of elevated stateliness. *Richard II* is not a play of action but of ceremonial, considered, gesture and posture. Such a quality of stance and movement comes from the compression of powerful feeling and concentrated meaning in a situation in which action is not possible, or will not lead anywhere. You cannot pass on the energy of feeling by which you are driven, you can only express it.

The point needs considering because the 'stateliness' of the play is puzzling when you are used to look for motive and consequence of action and points of view from which judgement is to be made or is being made. The tradition provided by the 'psychological' or 'realist' novel does not prepare us well for this kind of drama. The point I am making can be seen early, in Queen Isabel's distress:

> BUSHY Despair not, madam.
> QUEEN ISABEL   Who shall hinder me?
> I will despair and be at enmity
> With cozening hope. He is a flatterer,
> A parasite, a keeper-back of death
> Who gently would dissolve the bands of life
> Which false hope lingers in extremity
>
> (II.2.67–72)

These lines are bare of the kind of rich and startling imagery we perhaps think characteristic of Shakespeare, at least of the great tragedies. Simple personification and a restraint in vocabulary remarkable at such a moment (though not remarkable for the play) sets out with unanswerable clarity the hopelessness of the Queen's position. We have already seen, in the painful exchange between John of Gaunt and the Duchess of Gloucester, how this world is run by the men. There is nothing the Duchess can do to avenge her husband's murder unless she can get a man to do it for her. Similarly, the Queen is a bystander at the events of the play. She is passive, not in the sense of being docile, but rendered powerless by the position women have in this society.

Her meaning is terrible, and much more powerful if we see it not as the hyperbole of frustration and anger, but as a measured statement. Hope, she says, is like a flatterer, keeping us from the truth, and thus persuading us to keep on living. Our culture so emphasises the value of living that it may seem pathological to speak like this, but if we try to imagine the Queen's life at this point we see that there is nothing left. Like a good chess player who can see when a game cannot be won, she has resigned her position. Hope is for those who cannot see so clearly. Perhaps she means Bushy, as one of Richard's flatterers, to take the rebuke, or perhaps it is an irony the sharpness of which she means only to feel herself, but the audience gets a grim insight into a world of duplicity, lying, deceitful illusions, and can see that, once you have seen through it, you might have no will to live on. Richard can muster armies, but all the Queen can do is talk.

There are moments when all Shakespeare's great characters 'see'. Nothing happens, they just understand, and they make speeches in which they work out what they see, like Macbeth's great 'Tomorrow, and tomorrow, and tomorrow' (V.5.19ff), or Cleopatra's plangent dreams of Antony, 'I dreamt there was an Emperor Antony' (V.2.76ff). Then, in a sense, it is all over. This is the climax of these plays, but it is the predominant tone of *Richard II*. It is a play of speeches, even of set-pieces, such as John of Gaunt's encomium on England with which we began. These speeches 'celebrate' something, they concentrate and express something abstract and diffused, they 'enact' meaning, as ritual or symbol 'enacts' meaning. What they are about is brought into being for mind and feeling as experience, as reality, and here we may find the meaning of 'sceptred', not only what it means, but why it means.

The sceptre is the ceremonial sign of the rule of the king. This is not only his right to rule, but the rightfulness of his rule, the 'kingliness' of his being king. A king can be an almost sacred figure, deriving extraordinary power from his position as 'God's deputy':

> . . . the figure of God's majesty,
> His captain, steward, deputy elect,
> Anointed, crownèd . . .

(IV.1.125–127)

but it is a terrible mistake to confuse the person with the position.

It is easily done, because the king is supposed (in both senses) to express the position in his person, to be 'kingly'. The position exists separately, symbolised by the throne, the crown, the sceptre, but is not actualised until someone steps into the space created by the symbols (rather as, in the legend, only the true king can draw Excalibur from the stone). The king is limited always by what his subjects (especially the most powerful) regard as 'kingliness'. This is what is at issue in John of Gaunt's speech.

For John of Gaunt, 'sceptred' is tied up with peace and prosperity:

> This fortress built by nature for herself
> Against infection and the hand of war
>
> (II.1.43–44)

He is not denying that England is peaceful; however, he is criticising the conditions on which that peace has been bought:

> This land of such dear souls, this dear dear land,
> Dear for her reputation through the world,
> Is now leased out — I die pronouncing it —
> Like to a tenement or pelting farm.
>
> (II.1.57–60)

The rhythms of his speech reach a pitch with the phrase 'leased out', stressed by the pause that follows it and the emphatic phrase 'I die pronouncing it', and subside into its contemptuous concluding simile. Peace is not the only consideration.

Peace is what Richard protests he is trying to maintain in the face of the quarrel between Bolingbroke and Mowbray, and it is the keynote in his speech banishing them both, in which he describes the peace of England as his, expressing an almost mystical sense of the nation embodied in his person as king:

> To wake our peace, which in our country's cradle
> Draws the sweet infant-breath of gentle sleep
>
> (I.3.132–133)

It is clear though that Richard's mistake is to try to prevent Mowbray and Bolingbroke from meeting in a trial by combat.

Everything flows from this. His claim to be speaking and acting in the interests of peace runs up against the accusation that the 'kingliness' that should express England, 'This royal throne of kings . . . This nurse, this teeming womb of royal kings', has been 'leased out'. John of Gaunt shows a warrior's contempt for the doings of lawyers, 'inky blots and rotten parchment bonds', the material signs of 'leasing'. He speaks for right of possession by rightful force of arms. Though he speaks of peace, he seems to mean the peace of victory.

This perhaps reminds us that the sceptre is a symbolic weapon, and qualifies the ideal of peace with the ideal of honourable peace. Both this and the plea for the right to trial by combat have underpinning them the view that right will out in combat, not in the modern sense that 'might makes right', which may mean only that the victors get to write the history, but meaning that things are so organised that the righteous will be victorious. By standing in the way of this process Richard is appearing to be obstructing justice.

It is time to qualify the parallel I drew earlier between the tone of the tragedies and the tone of *Richard II*. In the climaxes of the tragedies no action is possible, but in the early part of *Richard II* action is prevented. The stateliness I have talked about is the experience of enforced inaction. This is imposed in the interests of Richard's idea of peace, which is simply the absence of hostilities. He invokes the spectre of armed conflict in harsh and vivid imagery in his speech banishing Bolingbroke and Mowbray, but it is clear that for John of Gaunt there is much more to peace and indeed Richard in pursuing his idea of peace has betrayed 'this sceptred isle'.

Richard's 'senseless conjuration' (III.2.4–26) offers, however, a powerful alternative, a passive, female, 'nature', to the active 'sceptre' of his enemies' imaginings of England. The activity of frogs and snakes notwithstanding, Richard is imagining nature as essentially supine. He is asking nature to be herself as it were more strongly. This is a paradox, and perhaps an insight into the inadequacy of Richard's idea against that of his opponents. Theirs is active and powerful in achievement: Richard's is fascinating in its passivity. In this sense the 'conjuration' is 'senseless', for Richard as magician is conjuring up something that cannot do anything. For an audience, though, the image has power, imaginative power: the brief glimpse of 'nature' is fascinating. It invites us to look and be quiet, to be attentive to the numerous goings-on of nature. His opponents invite us to take part in our imagination in the doing of decisive deeds. There is more to Richard's peace than a reluctance to act. His faith is in the 'golden crown' against which his enemies have raised 'shrewd steel' (III.2.59), and, as he describes the crown elsewhere as 'the hollow crown/ That rounds the mortal temples of a king' (III.2.160–161), we may take this figure of the crown and the sword as an opposition of 'female' and 'male' figures. 'Shrewd' is glossed for us when Richard meets Bolingbroke before Flint castle:

> Well you deserve. They well deserve to have
> That know the strongest and surest way to get.
>
> (III.3.200–201)

Richard identifies Bolingbroke with what we might call 'pragmatism' and which he calls 'policy' in a rueful remark to Queen Isabel when she is pleading with Northumberland to let Richard go with her into exile in France, 'That were some love, but little policy' (V.1.84).

Yet the Gardeners' scene qualifies this gathering identification of Richard with nature, passivity, and 'love'. The almost mystical identification of himself with the 'country' which threatens his sanity when he is deprived of the position of 'king' is brought into question by the image of the wise gardener. Richard's heart may have been in the right place, but he showed no sense of good management. He has not been a good gardener. On the other hand, Richard's 'nature' is not a garden. On the verge of madness, Richard comes to seem almost a holy fool, his love for his country not leading him to want to manage it but to give himself to it, in love.

History leaves Richard aside, pushing past him with a succession of incidents which show us the consequences of the view of kingship now in the ascendant. York doggedly sticks to an ideal of loyalty to the position, though it means prosecuting his own son. The paradox of his position would be comic if it were not horrifying. It was York who spoke so fervently against Bolingbroke's challenge to Richard, and who now urges the same man not to forgive his own son. This is the logic of loyalty to the position. Bolingbroke's own kingship is shown by his promise that a bewildering number of challenges will all be assigned their days of trial, and by the strangely distant disapproval he shows to Exton. There is no passion about King Henry. However, though he seems to be well able to avoid the mistakes Richard made, there is a disquieting parallelism about the beginning of the end of Richard's reign, and the beginning of Henry's reign. Richard's murder may seem a belated answer to Gloucester's murder, or an unsettling echo. As an echo, it undermines any feeling we may have that 'this sceptred isle' has settled its affairs and found the king to express its unity. Rather the feeling is of the banishing of one lot of ideas of England which proved untenable by another lot which probably will prove no more tenable. The play, though full of ideas of England, seems to settle on none. It is as though the place were unregenerately heterogeneous, undecidable, yet proved irresistibly tempting to define, especially for those, like John of Gaunt and Richard of Bordeaux who had come, in one way or another, from somewhere else. Perhaps the place only becomes clear for those, like Thomas Mowbray, who are leaving it for ever. It is hard to resist the complex, possibly cynical ambiguity of the familiar announcement of the passing of the sceptre:

The King is dead. Long live the King.

If this is so then we may see the deepest conflict of the play as being between the passionate need to assert the symbol, the sceptre, and a desperate inability to give it any fixed meaning. In this impasse there is no movement, nothing to be done, just the endless shaping of speech, if only to oneself.

AFTERTHOUGHTS

1

What significance does Potter attach in this essay to the word 'sceptred'?

2

What do you understand by 'the language of definition and self-definition' (page 21)?

3

Do you agree that Richard's fundamental error is 'to try to prevent Mowbray and Bolingbroke from meeting in a trial by combat' (page 25)?

4

Compare Potter's comments in this essay about the presentation of England in *Richard II* with the essays by Holderness (pages 53–63) and by Devlin (pages 65–77).

John E Cunningham

John E Cunningham currently divides his time between writing and travel. He is the author of numerous critical studies.

ESSAY

Bolingbroke: the emptier bucket?

During the deposition scene as he and Bolingbroke are holding the crown, Richard likens it to a well with two buckets: the emptier, his cousin, dances in the air while the other, full of water, is himself full of tears. Critics of the play have been quite ready to extend the image to their assessment of Bolingbroke's character, to see him as a mere lay-figure, an opportunist and no more, a man who is never seen to rule firmly or to be forceful. A kinder view is that the role is just a sketch for the character that is to be fully developed in the two plays — *Henry IV, Part 1* and *Henry IV, Part 2* — to which he gives his name as king. While a reading of the play shows at once that Richard has far more opportunity to reveal himself, his part being much longer, and after a performance it is his tragic figure that we are most likely to remember, a careful examination will perhaps show us that there is more in the bucket than at first appears.

Before we begin to look at the presentation of the future Henry IV it is as well to remind ourselves that Shakespeare had the greatest difficulty in putting this story on the stage at all. The monarch, it was firmly believed, ruled under God: to act against the monarch was treason, a crime not only against the man or woman, not only against the whole state, but against the

Creator, punishable by the most gruesome form of public execution. To show in public action the deposition of a rightful king by a usurper, even if the events were two centuries old, was to put yourself in real danger. As we shall see, Shakespeare is mindful of the risk and deliberately plays down some parts of the story, perhaps plays down the role of Bolingbroke himself. Even though the action ends in 1399, elderly men in the first audience would remember the time when Elizabeth's claim to the throne had been shaky, while younger ones might wonder what would happen to the succession when she died, as she was obviously going to, without issue. She survived this play in fact by less than a decade.

Henry IV ruled a little longer than that. Shakespeare made his reign, which lasted 14 years, a kind of link between that of Richard II, in which everything goes wrong and that of Henry V, in which everything is put right again — Bolingbroke's son, at the end of the play devoted to him, has won the splendid victory of Agincourt, made a good tactical marriage with the French royal family, restored peace: he has made amends for the wrong route by which his father came to the throne. But it would be a mistake to see Bolingbroke only as a link between two contrasting reigns. Acknowledging that his creator had to show him in a slightly ambiguous way, as a kind of honourable traitor, we can now turn to the play and see how his character is unfolded to us.

His very first words, often a key to a role, are:

> Many years of happy days befall
> My gracious sovereign, my most loving liege!

(I.1.20–21)

This establishes him as a loyal subject and one personally well disposed towards his cousin; the use of 'liege' is no accident, reminding us of the ancient duty of subject to sovereign. This loyalty, which is shortly to be stressed much more heavily, is almost immediately linked with great personal courage. In his forthright statement of why he comes as an appellant — it is he who has initiated the action, given the challenge — he asserts 'for what I speak/ My body shall make good upon this earth' (I.1.36–37) which reminds us that he proposes a combat to the death.

Having thrown down the gage that symbolises the challenge, Bolingbroke enlarges on his reasons. Mowbray, he says, has diverted a large sum of the king's money 'for lewd employments' and has been the fountainhead of every treasonable plot in the country for the last 18 years; above all, he contrived the death of Richard's uncle, the Duke of Gloucester, whose blood cries out to be avenged. Bolingbroke, then, is seen as one who fights against corruption, against treason, against murder of a relative.

This last point needed very careful handling. Shakespeare knew, and the better informed amongst his audience would know, that Richard had smarted for years under the domination of his uncle, having come to the throne very young. Gloucester died at Calais while in the custody of Mowbray. It was suspected that the King was a party to the murder. Here was another problem for an author — to show a rightful king guilty of murdering his own family. Shakespeare tucks away the evidence in a brief reference in the next scene, when Gaunt says:

> God's is the quarrel; for God's substitute,
> His deputy anointed in His sight,
> Hath caused his death

(I.2.37–39)

which makes Richard's guilt clear. Thus the whole of his treatment of Mowbray takes on a different appearance: he tries to stop the appeal altogether, not wishing the matter to be aired, then banishes for life the man who presumably acted on his orders. Even Mowbray dare not accuse the King himself of complicity, but he is safer out of the way. So the loyalty which Bolingbroke so earnestly and bravely shows is already to be seen as given to someone scarcely worthy of it. This is also seen in the way the first scene ends: Richard gives an order which is quite simply disobeyed — the best he can do is postpone the issue. Bolingbroke's reasons for disobeying complete our first impression of him. He says:

> Shall I seem crest-fallen in my father's sight?
> Or with pale beggar-fear impeach my height
> Before this out-dared dastard?

(I.1.188–190)

So far we have seen him as loyal, courageous, a man who is ready to set his life against corruption and treason: now he is shown as someone who will defy even his sovereign in the cause of personal honour.

To this formidable combination of strengths, the second scene, to which we have already referred, adds a strong suggestion that he is fighting in the right cause — and that the King knows it. So when he presents himself for battle it is, so to speak, with our support. Yet even in the formalities which precede the combat, Shakespeare has taken the opportunity to add to his stature. He asks leave to 'kiss my sovereign's hand' (I.3.46) before he fights, but Richard reminds him and us that they are of the same family — 'Farewell, my blood' (I.3.57). Bolingbroke goes on to take his leave of the Marshal, Aumerle and especially of his father, reminding us of how important family honour is to him and in sharp contrast with the way in which Richard is to treat his dying uncle a scene later. He leaves the stage for battle calling upon the patron saint of England and invoking what is surely never in doubt, his innocence.

His bold and forthright personality is thus in clear distinction from the way in which Richard now behaves. Having once ordered the disputants to be reconciled, without effect, having called them to Coventry, having sent them out to fight, he then changes his mind, calls them back, banishes them, but not for the same period of time, then changes his mind again and shortens Bolingbroke's sentence by nearly half. The reflection on this — 'such is the breath of kings' (I.3.215) — is the first hint we have that Bolingbroke sees his King as anything less than perfect; it may even suggest a kind of ambition, depending on how it is delivered. After a touching farewell to his father, he leaves the stage asserting in a ringing couplet that he is a true-born Englishman, and, as we have seen, his creator has been at some pains to make us accept this description. The flippant scene which follows, in which the King and his minions joke about his departure, reveals that the unseen audience, the common people, also approve of him and sneeringly implies that he debases himself to create a spurious popularity: this is quite contrary to the impression we have ourselves been given.

Presented to us as a man of high personal honour, Boling-broke now leaves the stage for three scenes, one of which is largely occupied by his father's death and Richard's summary taking-over of the Lancastrian estates. When he returns, in the third scene of Act II, he is significantly quiet: most of the talking is done by Northumberland, who is clearly a man on the make, and by York, a tired old fusspot who has been left, almost as a joke, in charge of the realm, a task he is manifestly impotent to undertake. Bolingbroke does however have one substantial speech — 'As I was banished, I was banished Hereford' (II.3.112ff) which is of great importance to our understanding of his motives. It is a plea for the supreme right of a man to inherit what is his. The crime — it would be seen as no less — of which Richard is guilty, which has brought this loyal exile back in defiance of sentence, is the stealing of his lands to finance an Irish expedition. Bolingbroke really has a right to claim his own and that helps us to accept it when he claims what is not his, the throne, though we may reflect that Richard has no heirs: by the laws of English succession, on his death the crown should have passed to the children of his uncle, the Duke of Clarence, though these were all girls and it would have needed a woman as remarkable as Elizabeth herself to take hold of this unruly kingdom of men. In fact at the end of the scene Bolingbroke is already taking upon himself a duty which the King should rightly have carried out — to purge the realm of the 'caterpillars of the commonwealth' (II.3.165) and that is what we see him doing next.

The condemnation of Bushy and Green, with which the third Act opens, is a foretaste of his kingship. He is not only dealing out justice with great firmness — a strong contrast with Richard's capricious behaviour — but he is giving his reasons. These men have corrupted the King — even sexually perverted him, it seems — as well as appropriated Bolingbroke's estates and fouled his name. Yet if his sentence seems to us severe we must not only remember that when the play was written penalties were ferocious, but also consider the way the scene ends. The Queen to whom these men have brought such grief is to be treated with care and compassion. Though he leaves the stage to fight, our impression is of a man still essentially loyal — and royal.

For many people the deposition scene is the heart of the play, the great confrontation between the cousins. More crucial, surely, is the scene in the base court of Flint Castle, at the end of which Richard is a prisoner and Bolingbroke is in charge of him and, effectively, the country. Shakespeare has to tread as warily here as in the handing over of the crown.

His method is one which encourages those who see Bolingbroke as a negative character to press their case. In effect, Richard offers himself as a prisoner, or at least as a man defeated, before there is any sign of force. In the scene before that which takes place at Flint, Richard talks himself into despair, refusing the efforts of his little band of friends to hearten him, dismissing the troops that remain:

> That power I have, discharge, and let them go
> To ear the land that hath some hope to grow;
> For I have none.

> (III.2.211–213)

And in this spirit of hopelessness he goes to Flint to 'pine away' as he puts it.

Bolingbroke's approach to Flint is scrupulously correct. He sends a herald with a message of his own allegiance, says he will lay down his arms at Richard's feet provided that his lands are restored. He orders his troops to march 'without the noise of threatening drum' (III.3.51) and in no way offers force or violence. What happens after that is that Richard, already determined that he is finished with kingship, talks himself into surrender:

> What must the King do now? Must he submit?
> The King shall do it. Must he be deposed?
> The King shall be contented. Must he lose
> The name of king? A God's name, let it go.

> (III.3.143–146)

It is scarcely fair to charge Bolingbroke with 'inertia' as one critic has done, when Richard answers his own questions in this way. The moment of decision for Bolingbroke falls at the very end of this scene, when Richard says to him:

> What you will have, I'll give, and willing too;
> For do we must what force will have us do.
> Set on towards London, cousin — is it so?

> (III.3.206–208)

And Bolingbroke simply has to acquiesce. There has been no show of 'force' and he has steadfastly said that he comes only to claim his own: what is implicit in the scene is that Richard has renounced his throne and his cousin must take it if the country is to be saved from anarchy.

A similar pattern may be found in the deposition scene, but Bolingbroke's character is further strengthened by the episode which precedes it, the quarrel between the nobles and the throwing down of the gages. This is often cut in performance because it is awkward — the repeated casting of gloves can make an audience giggle, however careful the production — but if it is cut we lose something of Bolingbroke and something of the artistic symmetry of the play. This passage is a deliberate echo of the opening, also a quarrelsome challenge in the presence of authority.

There are two differences, however. One is in the size of the uproar, the general impression being that half the court, not just two men, are at each other's throats: the other is the bearing of the man before whom they are challenging one another. Richard notably demonstrates his inability to make Bolingbroke and Mowbray patch up their quarrel, but Bolingbroke, in command from the very beginning, where he orders Bagot to speak out, quietly waits until they have done, then authoritatively puts them all under arrest, with sureties. There is a further echo of the first scene in that Mowbray is mentioned, and Bolingbroke shows another quality, which is to be emphasised in the last Act, that of magnanimity. Bolingbroke declares that, although the man was his enemy, he is to be repealed and have his lands restored to him. We remember that it was the theft, by Richard, of Gaunt's lands that brought his son back to England. Then York, as Richard's spokesman, invites Henry to ascend the throne with the King's good will: in fact he says that Richard has adopted Bolingbroke as his heir.

This moment is of double significance. It puts Bolingbroke in the right, as it were, before ever Richard appears, and it also puts him physically on the throne: for the remaining two-thirds of this major scene Henry is in a position of literal superiority, watching Richard acting out the strange and moving pantomime or ritual, according to how we see him, of abdication. On stage — and Shakespeare wrote for the theatre, not the study — the quiet but commanding presence of the new king is highly impressive. Richard, always inclined to dramatise himself, performs to the court, and, having played his part, goes away, leaving Bolingbroke as he was from the beginning, in charge. Bolingbroke's first action as a king may also be seen in this passage — Northumberland, already showing signs of the arrogance that was later to lead him into open rebellion, keeps trying to insist that Richard read a recantation of his supposed 'crimes' and is told to desist: though he gives a surly answer, the matter is not pursued, for Henry is a king who means to be obeyed.

The Act ends with the first rumbles of trouble for the new monarchy, but also with a clear sense of there now being a strong, brave and generous-spirited man on the throne, freely given to him. What does Shakespeare still have to do? In a way the question is answered for us by the Duke of York telling his wife of the triumphal entry of Bolingbroke to London (V.2). This speaks of his enormous popularity, and we might wonder why he is so well liked by ordinary folk, for though we have seen him to have many virtues, this is not to make him particularly 'human' — a collection of good qualities is not enough, in itself, to make a complete character with whom the audience can feel in sympathy. Bolingbroke's more human side is shown with economy and wit — the play is notably lacking in humour elsewhere — in the third scene of Act V. This begins with a picture of Henry as a man and father having trouble, as fathers do, with his son. His son, as sons will, sends a very rude answer to his parent's celebrations: he says he will take a glove from the cheapest tart in the red-light district and wear that as his favour in the coming triumphs — a typical bit of youthful showing off with its emphasis on his own sexual maturity. Interestingly that is just how his father sees it:

> As dissolute as desperate. Yet through both
> I see some sparks of better hope, which elder years
> May happily bring forth.

(V.3.20–22)

Then Bolingbroke has to deal with York, already established as a sadly hen-pecked man by the episode of the boots. Faced with two loyal old parties, both on their knees — York loyal to him, the Duchess to her son — quarrelling with all the fervour of a long marriage to draw on, and yet with a quite serious matter behind it, a plot to kill the King no less — faced with this situation, embarrassing in every way, Bolingbroke deals with it courteously and above all with kindness. Aumerle is young, like his own son, and is pardoned, though older heads that are involved are to fall.

Not all of them, however; for in the final scene of the play, he shows mercy to Carlisle, who had at least the honesty to voice his protest in public, in a major speech in the deposition scene, before resorting to other means. He is allowed honourable retirement, others are executed, rebellion is put down. Almost his last act is to show that he can be grateful to those who have served him — not a quality we can ever take for granted — as he thanks and promises rewards to Northumberland and Fitzwater. One man only expects thanks and gets none: Exton.

Bolingbroke's final speech, the last of the play, directed at the assassin and then to his court, is no trite finale. Without any hesitation he accepts guilt: 'I did wish him dead' (V.6.39) he says bluntly and goes on to speak of his 'guilty hand'. His concern here — and it is the last touch in his portrait — is not to excuse himself but to atone by making a solemn pilgrimage. When he says he 'loves' the murdered man we may recall that that was always his position: we may also recall that Richard, apart from one short scene in which he says farewell to a queen he had not treated well, never shows signs of loving anyone but himself. He surely is the emptier bucket.

1

How would *you* advise an actor to deliver the line 'such is the breath of kings' (page 33)?

2

How acceptable do you find it for a director of a Shakespeare play to cut individual episodes or scenes (see page 36)?

3

Do you agree that the end of Act IV gives 'a clear sense of there now being a strong, brave and generous-spirited man on the throne' (page 37)?

4

Do you accept that Bolingbroke 'loves' the murdered man (page 38)?

Stephen Hazell

Stephen Hazell is Deputy Principal at the Central School of Speech and Drama, London.

ESSAY

Personal authority in *Richard II*

'Can no man tell me of my unthrifty son?', Bolingbroke asks towards the end of *Richard II* (V.3.1). The word 'thrift' is complex. It has to do with 'profit' in the sense of making good use of what one is given. Bolingbroke's complaint is only partly that his son Henry is wasting money in taverns. The account being reckoned is ethical also; Bolingbroke laments that his son is a 'young wanton, and effeminate boy' who is making it a point of honour to support a 'dissolute crew' (V.3.10–12). Had he possessed prophetic powers, Bolingbroke would have stopped worrying: Henry is Prince Hal, due to become Henry V, the most heroic of the pageant of English kings. Prince Hal, it becomes clear in *Henry IV, Part 1* has a life-plan: he'll lead people to believe that he's a bad lot and then, when the moment to assert himself comes, he will appear as a changed man, publicly reject the dissolute crew (in the figure of Falstaff), and take the king-ship by storm. This plan is revealed in soliloquy long before it is put into effect:

> So when this loose behaviour I throw off,
> And pay the debt I never promised,
> By how much better than my word I am,

I'll so offend, to make offence a skill,
Redeeming time when men think least I will.

(*1 Henry IV*, I.2.206–208, 214–215)

In making time good and paying debts, he will prove a thrifty
son. The unthrifty son of our play is Richard himself.

Richard recognises at the end that: 'I wasted time, and now
doth time waste me' (V.5.49); and all through the play others
point up his mis-spending. Northumberland wants to 'Redeem
from broking pawn the blemished crown' (II.1.293), and York
contrasts Richard's father with Richard himself, to his face:

His noble hand
Did win what he did spend, and spent not that
Which his triumphant father's hand had won.

(II.1.179–181)

Prince Hal makes good; Richard wastes. And they both do it in
the context of family rivalries: these rivalries, between cousins,
brothers, and fathers and sons, feel like the most important
single psychological and political feature of Shakespeare's
sequence of English history plays.

In Prince Hal's case — *1 Henry IV* — there is most obviously
the rivalry with Hotspur as the other up-and-coming leadership
figure: Bolingbroke fears Hal will be set aside. Hotspur is all
shining courage — but he has no negotiating or planning
talents, and in the event Hal not only defeats him diplomati-
cally, but in hand-to-hand combat as well. The more interesting
rivalry is with his father. This is symbolised in the scene where
he steals the crown from his sleeping father's head to try it on
for size; he does not wish his father's death, but that death is
a necessary step to his own inheritance of the crown, and it is
part of his plan that he shall be seen as a new-born king, not
a prolonger of the old regime. As children must, in order to
become effective adults, both find models of adulthood in their
parents *and* separate themselves from those parents, so princes
must both emulate and defeat their father-rivals.

There is a teasing absence in Shakespeare's play of any
detailed account of the relationship between Richard and his
father; the clearest view we get is from York in the speech
quoted earlier, and it's worth giving at greater length:

emptiness' because that seems to be crucial. We do not see this at first. Acts I and II give us Richard's style of operation as king before the rivalry challenge from Bolingbroke leads to the exposure of his profound inner doubts. It is the Queen who fore-shadows the state of mind for the audience in II.2; she is already struck with a sense of foreboding, a feeling that there will be much to grieve at, though the only cause she has so far is Richard's departure for Ireland:

> Yet again methinks
> Some unborn sorrow ripe in fortune's womb
> Is coming towards me, and my inward soul
> With nothing trembles. At something it grieves
> More than with parting from my lord the King.
>
> (II.2.9–13)

Her 'inward soul', her intuition as we would call it (and she uses the identical phrase at line 28), has seen something disturbing, and it's hard to see what her intuition could concern except some quality in Richard, the whole of her concentration is on her 'sweet' husband, and not at all on the political situation. In searching for what's wrong within her, she finds herself consistently playing with the idea of nothing, summed up perhaps in the line: 'For nothing hath begot my something grief' (line 36). There is an absence where there should be some strong reassurance and from this the grief is born, the 'nameless woe' (line 40). This feeling, which we've probably all experienced, of a deep stomach-churning but inexplicable doubt, prepares the audience's mind for what they are to find in Richard. It can be noted that, to the end, Isabel sees Richard as a king of sorrows:

> But soft, but see, or rather do not see,
> My fair rose wither. Yet look up, behold,
> That you in pity may dissolve to dew
> And wash him fresh again with true-love tears.
> . . .
>
> . . . Thou most beauteous inn,
> Why should hard-favoured grief be lodged in thee
> When triumph is become an alehouse guest?
>
> (V.1.7–10, 13–15)

Richard is seen as beautiful but with sorrow as a permanent

inner guest, whereas success dwells with the common, down-to-earth 'alehouse' Bolingbroke.

Richard's return from Ireland is prefaced by Salisbury's tear-filled prophecy:

> I see thy glory like a shooting star
> Fall to the base earth from the firmament.
> Thy sun sets weeping in the lowly west

(II.4.19–21)

and Richard, on landing, greets his kingdom with:

> As a long-parted mother with her child
> Plays fondly with her tears and smiles in meeting,
> So weeping, smiling, greet I thee, my earth,
> And do thee favours with my royal hands.
> Feed not thy sovereign's foe, my gentle earth

(III.2.8–12)

A father (king) whose child (kingdom) is threatened by a family rival would usually act; fatherhood confers a supremely powerful authority for action. But Richard's inner incapacity for this role is evidenced in his choice of 'mother' for his self-image, a mother, at that, who feels the most she can do is to plead with her child not to betray her.

On provocation from the supporters around him, Richard from time to time rouses himself to play-act the role of king, but the performance lacks conviction; an inner sense of powerlessness appears to be the fundamental truth. A display of tears is then his main consolation, weapon, or source of action — and even the action has a fantasy quality. Consider the following examples:

> Make dust our paper, and with rainy eyes
> Write sorrow on the bosom of the earth.

(III.2.146–147)

(Note that the earth now, with its bosom, is mother rather than child, Richard covering with tears its unsustaining breasts; Richard feels orphaned almost, lacking a supporting parent.)

> We'll make foul weather with despisèd tears.

(III.3.161)

(Richard beats down, in his imagination, the crops in his kingdom with tears, and goes on to make graves with the unceasing fall of those tears; his grief leads him to thoughts of sterility and death.)

> Mine eyes are full of tears, I cannot see.
> And yet salt water blinds them not so much
> But they can see a sort of traitors here.

(IV.1.243–245)

(Richard, his kingship now given to Bolingbroke and so in all ways powerless, seeks consolation in blaming others, for betrayal.)

It looks, then, accurate enough to perceive Richard as lacking in inner authority, without an inner adult model to motivate action as a king. Often, this comes close to his lacking a sense of self altogether, to feeling nothing at the centre — the nothing which has begotten his Queen's something grief. The most obvious image of this is that which stands as the central image of the whole play — the 'hollow crown' (III.2.160). To Richard, the crown has come to feel not like the awesome symbol of majesty and authority, but a golden mockery: within it, there is only emptiness. The passage from IV.1 quoted in the previous paragraph is immediately followed by a discourse on his loss of identity.

> No lord of thine, thou haught insulting man;
> Nor no man's lord. I have no name, no title —
> No, not that name was given me at the font —
> But 'tis usurped.

(IV.1.253–256)

'Richard' sounds meaninglessly in his ears, if it cannot be 'King Richard'. As king he has only been able to play 'a little scene' (III.2.164) and as a private human being he cannot find himself at all. His fantasising in prison at the end is the logical conclusion of his emotional distress at lack of self:

> Sometimes am I king.
> Then treasons make me wish myself a beggar;
> And so I am. Then crushing penury
> Persuades me I was better when a king.

> Then am I kinged again; and by and by
> Think that I am unkinged by Bolingbroke,
> And straight am nothing. But whate'er I be,
> Nor I, nor any man that but man is,
> With nothing shall be pleased till he be eased
> With being nothing.

(V.5.32–41)

His inner life mercilessly circles round his failed kingship and the emptiness which threatens when he is only himself; so much so that by now the only rest for his broken mind is the promise of death — 'being nothing'.

This is a deeply tragic portrait; our curve of experience of the play is, I would think, from impatience and even anger with Richard to a shocked and moved understanding. It is worth now taking a retrospective look at the earlier parts of the play.

The first scene presents us with a trial, ostensibly of Mowbray, with Bolingbroke as the accuser and Richard and the state elders as judges. Richard appears to be playing his part, in control:

> Then call them to our presence. Face to face,
> And frowning brow to brow, ourselves will hear
> The accuser and the accusèd freely speak.

(I.1.15–17)

Bolingbroke's most significant accusation is that Mowbray 'did plot the Duke of Gloucester's death' (line 100). Mowbray's answer to this is indirect and odd, presumably because of the company: 'I slew him not, but to my own disgrace/ Neglected my sworn duty in that case' (lines 133–134). He can only be saying that his sworn duty (that is, to Richard) would have been to kill Gloucester himself rather than leave it to others, but he is leaving the account obscure so that he cannot be made to say directly that the murder was ultimately Richard's responsibility. Gaunt, in his plain-speaking way, makes matters clear when he says to Richard later that Gloucester's death stands as good witness 'That thou respectest not spilling Edward's blood' (II.2.131) — i.e. that he hasn't stopped short of murder in seeking to destroy his grandfather Edward's son. (See also I.2.37–39.) Mowbray shows his feeling of betrayal when banished for life ('A heavy sentence, my most sovereign liege,/ And all unlooked-for from your highness' mouth' — I.3.154–155). Progressively we are drawn to see Richard as the in-fact guilty party for Gloucester's death — and so it is he, not Mowbray, who is really on trial.

Richard makes an early, and unconvincingly offhand, bid for the whole matter to be put behind them:

> Forget, forgive, conclude, and be agreed;
> Our doctors say this is no month to bleed.

(I.1.156–157)

This won't wash with the protagonists who see there has to be a real resolution to a major political conflict, and so Richard has to put the matter to trial by combat. His most effective action of the play is to arrange matters so that both men get banished — it's not a solution, but it buys him time. He is, of course, already the prisoner of his blood-spilling past. Having once tried to establish himself within the family rivalries by having an opponent made away with (and I think this should be seen as an act of weakness rather than strength), he can only confirm his position by further ruthlessness. So the time he buys is in order to find other ways of neutralising the threat from Bolingbroke; he reveals a little of his hand to Aumerle:

> He is our cousin, cousin, but 'tis doubt,
> When time shall call him home from banishment,
> Whether our kinsman come to see his friends.

(I.4.20–23)

Richard's track-record suggests another murder-plot may be in the shaping; in the event, Bolingbroke is already on his way back before Richard returns from Ireland. The Richard of the earlier part of this play, then, is impatient with negotiation and easily tempted, when confronted with problems from political rivals, by the impulsive brutal solution. This comes through most shockingly as soon as he hears of Gaunt's illness:

> Now put it, God, in the physician's mind
> To help him to his grave immediately!
> The lining of his coffers shall make coats
> To deck our soldiers for these Irish wars.

(I.4.59–62)

This is government by impulse, not by true authority.

As so often in Shakespeare, a journey and the return from it constitute a dividing point in the structure of the play (the Hamlet who returns to Denmark from England, for example, is changed). The journey for Richard is that to Ireland, and occurs quite early in the play. Beforehand, he is not a good king — as we have seen, he is impulsive and immature — but he has not yet shown himself incapable of the exercise of power, even if he has not filled the role authoritatively. On his return, the test provided by the challenge that Bolingbroke's simultaneous return has thrown down, immediately appears too much for him, and the symptoms of the malaise that have been the main subject of this essay so far are, I would say, also the main subject of Shakespeare's presentation of Richard for the remainder of the play.

The sense of emptiness, and of inner powerlessness, and the tear-filled recognition of this which makes him depose himself and welcome the descent to nothingness, have already been drawn out. The other striking side of his conduct which can escape no one's notice is his theatricality and attention-seeking. He ensures that his grieving, distressed condition is in full display for its own sake, not with any apparent view to recovering himself and his position. His dramatisation of his plight reaches its highest moment of hysteria in the speech in III.3 beginning 'Down, down I come like glistering Phaethon' (line 178); it is a panic-filled acceptance of his inability to find the inner strength to overcome Bolingbroke, and leads shortly to:

> Cousin, I am too young to be your father
> Though you are old enough to be my heir.
> What you will have, I'll give, and willing too;
> For do we must what force will have us do.
> Set on towards London, cousin — is it so?

>   (III.3.204–208)

Had Richard a father's capacity within him he would draw on it now; all he has is a sense of being too young, and having, in the crucial encounters, to give way to those who have maturity enough. The question with which he ends this speech directly delivers his fate into Bolingbroke's hands — his complicity with the deposition is established, and the rest is just acting it out.

Act it out he does, with patience-stretching speeches and a playlet with a mirror. But the underlying content can only be self-pity for a condition of life that is without clear meaning or purpose to him. In prison, he reminds one of a man in a psychiatric ward, struggling hopelessly but repeatedly with thoughts of the pattern of his life. One image he achieves — though its oddity and complexity make it hard to unpick — is that his wiping a tear from his eye each minute is like a clock-hand moving endlessly across its face:

> My thoughts are minutes, and with sighs they jar
> Their watches on unto mine eyes, the outward watch,
> Whereto my finger, like a dial's point,
> Is pointing still in cleansing them from tears.
>
> (V.5.51–54)

'Still' means 'always'. Time is now nothing to him but the wiping of tears. There is a poignant sense of a man inescapably reduced to the endless repetition of a single signifying action. The centre of *Richard II* is an extraordinary portrait of the consequences for a man of his inability to achieve adulthood.

Richard's failure to integrate self and role lead to an experience of time as an exercise in counting merely, with no sense of significant movement. As I indicated at the beginning of the essay, the diametrically contrasting figure in the sequence of history plays is Prince Hal 'redeeming time' — finding a way to grow up into his role and to adapt his role to himself. In this play, the contrasting figure is Bolingbroke, whose ultimate success is more ordinary — impressive enough but incomplete. One example will serve here to point the contrast with Richard as to fathers — Bolingbroke's reasonably successful modelling on his father, while growing up independently. When he returns to England, York puts it to him that he is in rebellion against the sovereign and therefore against the very principle of legitimacy of inheritance upon which, in asking for his lands and title, he is claiming to act. He replies:

> You are my father; for methinks in you
> I see old Gaunt alive. O then, my father,
> Will you permit that I shall stand condemned

A wandering vagabond, my rights and royalties
Plucked from my arms perforce, and given away
To upstart unthrifts? Wherefore was I born?
. . .
What would you have me do? I am a subject,
And I challenge law. Attorneys are denied me,
And therefore personally I lay my claim
To my inheritance of free descent.

(II.3.116–121, 132–135)

He acknowledges his father as model — and adroitly appeals to York as his father's brother to take over the protective parental role — but equally insists that he is separate, grown-up, and hence able to act on his own for his rights. He significantly points to those who hold his lands as 'unthrifts' — as not making profitable use of an inheritance which is not rightly theirs anyway — and sees his life as necessarily purposeful. The cry 'wherefore was I born?' affords a rare glimpse of motivating passion into a character whose conduct usually appears well-calculated and unsparingly authoritative. He is a thrifty son and it is hard to deny, for the kingdom's sake, the validity of his ascent to the throne. He has though, an incompleteness — even he cannot find the full integrity for the role of king, and a continued insecurity leads to the voicing of a wish, a destructive impulse: 'Have I no friend will rid me of this living fear?' (V.4.2). His now-harmless cousin, wiping away the minutes in his prison cell, is to be done away with. Bolingbroke also has blood on his hands at the beginning of his reign. His case is quite different from Richard's, however, and *1* and *2 Henry IV* show a different balance-sheet of success and failure in Henry Bolingbroke's management of his grown-up life.

AFTERTHOUGHTS

1

Do you agree that children need to find models of adulthood in their parents in order to become 'effective' adults (page 41)?

2

Do you agree that there would be a 'good deal' to say for Richard as husband or companion (page 43)?

3

Why does Hazell judge the 'hollow crown' to be the central image of *Richard II* (page 46)? Do you agree with his interpretation?

4

What do you understand by 'Richard's failure to integrate self and role' (page 50)?

Graham Holderness

*Graham Holderness is Head of the
Drama Department at the Roehampton
Institute of Higher Education, and has
published numerous works of criticism.*

ESSAY

'A woman's war': femininity in *Richard II*

In one of the key scenes of *Richard II*, that which contains the play's best-known speech — John of Gaunt's famous patriotic celebration of 'this earth, this realm, this England' — King Richard marks his departure from the stage by speaking, almost as an afterthought, to his Queen Isabel:

> Come on, our Queen; tomorrow must we part.
> Be merry; for our time of stay is short.

(II. 1. 222–223)

A reader of the printed play-text (as distinct from the spectator of a performance) could be forgiven for wondering, at least momentarily, where this queen came from. She has not herself spoken or acted, nor has she been spoken or even referred to, in the course of the 150 or so lines during which she occupies the stage. It is actually necessary to look back to the stage-direction which announces the arrival of the King (at line 68) to see that the Queen enters with the King and a group of nobles. For the reader of the play (whose attention is necessarily focused on those characters who manifest their presence in speech), a silent, self-effacing character, who is also ignored by everyone else in the room, simply does not exist. In a stage particular historical character of this action excludes the active agency of women in a particularly decisive and intractable way, has rather more force than the other two. It is one thing to invent an interesting dramatic character for Isabel; but if women did not (outside romances like Spenser's *The Faerie Queene*), take part in chivalric combats, Shakespeare could hardly clap his Queen in armour and let her fight the King's battles for him. In the course of that elaborate exchange of formal speeches which constitutes the opening scene of the play, where Henry Bolingbroke accuses Thomas Mowbray of treason, Mowbray offers a useful commentary on this aspect of the matter:

> Let not my cold words here accuse my zeal.
> 'Tis not the trial of a woman's war,
> The bitter clamour of two eager tongues,
> Can arbitrate this cause betwixt us twain.
> The blood is hot that must be cooled for this.
>
> (I.1.47–51)

It is hard to imagine a more precise or more decisive definition of an absolute and irreconcilable difference between the sexes. Fighting, an active and positive enterprise, is done with the 'blood' and the body, and it can only be done by men. The only kind of fighting Mowbray can imagine women being involved in is a scolding squabble between 'two eager tongues'. The energy and vigour that characterise masculine militarism are absent from the latter activity: the woman's words are 'cold', while the warrior's blood is 'hot'. There is even a latent accusation of constitutional cowardice on the part of women, who are far more 'eager' to engage in the cold clamour of a verbal quarrel than they would be to undertake the physical challenge of a real battle. The patent substance of Mowbray's words is of course an accusation against Bolingbroke, tantamount to a charge of effeminacy: he (Mowbray) is too manly to join in this humiliating conflict of words, and cannot wait to get onto the field where the real 'trial' can begin. It will seem odd from our modern conceptions of law and justice that the value of words and of argument to a legal process should be so discredited: but that of course is the nature of a chivalric trial by combat. Both Mowbray's misogyny and his superstitious reliance on physical

Graham Holderness

*Graham Holderness is Head of the
Drama Department at the Roehampton
Institute of Higher Education, and has
published numerous works of criticism.*

ESSAY

'A woman's war: femininity in *Richard II*

In one of the key scenes of *Richard II*, that which contains the play's best-known speech — John of Gaunt's famous patriotic celebration of 'this earth, this realm, this England' — King Richard marks his departure from the stage by speaking, almost as an afterthought, to his Queen Isabel:

> Come on, our Queen; tomorrow must we part.
> Be merry; for our time of stay is short.

(II. 1. 222–223)

A reader of the printed play-text (as distinct from the spectator of a performance) could be forgiven for wondering, at least momentarily, where this queen came from. She has not herself spoken or acted, nor has she been spoken or even referred to, in the course of the 150 or so lines during which she occupies the stage. It is actually necessary to look back to the stage-direction which announces the arrival of the King (at line 68) to see that the Queen enters with the King and a group of nobles. For the reader of the play (whose attention is necessarily focused on those characters who manifest their presence in speech), a silent, self-effacing character, who is also ignored by everyone else in the room, simply does not exist. In a stage production of course things are different: the text calls for the Queen to be physically, visibly present among the King's entourage, and her silent, passive presence could actually be made quite significant. But when deciding what to do with the Queen, actors and directors are left entirely to their own devices, reliant on the resources of their own imaginations: for the verbal text itself has nothing whatsoever to say about the strange silent presence of Queen Isabel.

Scene II.1 involves eleven characters, only one of whom — the Queen — is female. That disproportionate marginalisation of the female population is typical of this play as a whole. Only five female characters appear in a cast of over thirty identified parts (not counting various supernumery servants, attendants, soldiers, who are also overwhelmingly male): these are the Duchess of Gloucester, who appears only in I.2 (her death is then reported in II.2, line 97); the Duchess of York, who appears only in V.2; and the Queen, who appears in three scenes — II.2, III.4, V.1. — in addition to her silent presence in II.1.

Now a number of common-sense arguments naturally present themselves to suggest that there is really nothing remarkable in this. There is never more than a handful of female parts in any of Shakespeare's plays; a fact obviously connected with the Elizabethan practice of using boys to play the roles of women. *Richard II* is a history play, and Elizabethan history plays were drawn from historical writings which did not particularly emphasise the presence or agency of women in history: history was largely thought of as an account of the actions of men. Lastly, this particular historical drama deals with the kind of political and military crises which necessarily excluded women from active participation: political struggles, trials by combat, military campaigns. That exclusion of women from the decisive and determinant activities of a society is something we would naturally, from the perspective of modern ideas, decry: but it is a historical injustice for which we can hardly blame Shakespeare. In the historical story of the deposition of Richard II, he found no remarkable or influential women: so that absence was duly and dutifully reflected in the play.

A moment's consideration will reveal that all these apparently 'common-sense' arguments are extremely suspect. It is a fact that only a small number of female roles is to be found in

Elizabethan plays. But the women characters who occupy those roles usually have a disproportionate influence within the world of the play: Viola, Rosalind, Portia; Cordelia, Desdemona, Lady Macbeth. It is even often the case that they show strengths and abilities, kinds of determination and resourcefulness, not displayed at all by their menfolk. As we witness Portia dominating and winning Antonio's trial in *The Merchant of Venice*, or Cordelia leading an army in *King Lear*, or Lady Macbeth stabbing Duncan's grooms in *Macbeth*, we are unlikely to derive from Shakespeare's plays any simple notion of women as 'the weaker sex'. This is certainly not the case in *Richard II*, where the Queen is a pathetic melancholy spectator of her husband's downfall.

The Elizabethan dramatist's relationship with his historical sources was not a passive and automatic subservience. Although the Tudor period saw the emergence of a modern conception of historical 'fact' (Samuel Daniel, author of a long poem about the Wars of the Roses, carefully distinguished between authentic historical fact and imaginative fiction) all the history plays of this period mingle fact with interpretation, historical authenticity with imaginative elaboration. When Shakespeare dramatised other periods of history in which women are described as having some kind of prominence, he gave them even more prominent roles in his plays — Joan of Arc and Queen Margaret in the *Henry VI* plays are obvious examples. After *Richard II* Shakespeare started to interpolate fictional comic sub-plots into the 'factual' material of the chronicle drama, thus providing more space for the participation of women: in the *Henry IV* plays, women like the Hostess and Doll Tearsheet have active and important (if distinctly 'low-life') roles to play. It was quite open to him to make more of Queen Isabel than the historical sources themselves warranted. In fact he did, since the young woman who appears in the play to express her unfocused melancholy, to complain of her husband's declining fortunes, and to lament his tragic overthrow, has no real historical authority at all: Isabel was a child of ten when these events occurred. Her passive role in the play is then, we might say, historically appropriate; her dramatic characterisation is all Shakespeare's invention.

The third argument from 'common sense', that the

particular historical character of this action excludes the active agency of women in a particularly decisive and intractable way, has rather more force than the other two. It is one thing to invent an interesting dramatic character for Isabel; but if women did not (outside romances like Spenser's *The Faerie Queene*), take part in chivalric combats, Shakespeare could hardly clap his Queen in armour and let her fight the King's battles for him. In the course of that elaborate exchange of formal speeches which constitutes the opening scene of the play, where Henry Bolingbroke accuses Thomas Mowbray of treason, Mowbray offers a useful commentary on this aspect of the matter:

> Let not my cold words here accuse my zeal.
> 'Tis not the trial of a woman's war,
> The bitter clamour of two eager tongues,
> Can arbitrate this cause betwixt us twain.
> The blood is hot that must be cooled for this.

(I.1.47–51)

It is hard to imagine a more precise or more decisive definition of an absolute and irreconcilable difference between the sexes. Fighting, an active and positive enterprise, is done with the 'blood' and the body, and it can only be done by men. The only kind of fighting Mowbray can imagine women being involved in is a scolding squabble between 'two eager tongues'. The energy and vigour that characterise masculine militarism are absent from the latter activity: the woman's words are 'cold', while the warrior's blood is 'hot'. There is even a latent accusation of constitutional cowardice on the part of women, who are far more 'eager' to engage in the cold clamour of a verbal quarrel than they would be to undertake the physical challenge of a real battle. The patent substance of Mowbray's words is of course an accusation against Bolingbroke, tantamount to a charge of effeminacy: he (Mowbray) is too manly to join in this humiliating conflict of words, and cannot wait to get onto the field where the real 'trial' can begin. It will seem odd from our modern conceptions of law and justice that the value of words and of argument to a legal process should be so discredited: but that of course is the nature of a chivalric trial by combat. Both Mowbray's misogyny and his superstitious reliance on physical force as a means of securing justice are clearly, to us (and were, in my view, to Shakespeare), visible as anachronisms; dated, old-fashioned, antiquated beliefs, belonging to a particular histori-cal society. Those active and enterprising heroines who appear in other Shakespeare plays seem to belong to an age when a formidable queen showed herself capable (in a sense) of fighting her own battles, such as that against the Spanish Armada; and they appear naturally sympathetic to our own later age in which the principle of female equality is, though hardly universally attained, at least generally accepted. Mowbray's words, and Isabel's character, belong rather to that post-feudal society of the late fourteenth century in which, according to the dominant systems of belief, men were warriors and women a protected species.

It seems to me possible that the marginalisation of women in a play like *Richard II* is not simply the symptomatic expression of an unconscious misogyny, or a passive reflection of pre-determined historical conditions. It is rather a historical reality, which the play foregrounds, interrogates and criticises. Women may not be much in evidence in the play, but feminity is. Let us take a closer look at the scene with which we began (II.1), the scene of Isabel's strangely absent presence. As I noted above, Isabel appears there in a scene populated otherwise entirely by men. The problems and issues debated in the scene are specifically 'masculine' preserves: politics, war, economics, law, property. Throughout the scene, what the characters say about their specific situation carries with it wider dimensions of reference, so that other groups of people are continually being alluded to and moving into temporary focus. Again, these are all groups of men. Young men, sick men, dying men, living men, flattering courtiers, lawyers, Englishmen ('this happy breed'), Frenchmen, Irishmen, fathers, grandfathers, brothers, sons, uncles, kings, knights, commons, nobles, ancestors, 'men of war'. It would be hard to imagine a world more thoroughly cleared of any sign of the female gender.

Yet if we look a little closer, vestigial traces of femininity begin to surface: the repressed returns. John of Gaunt sings the praises of that 'happy breed of men' (II.1.45) who under the strong government of warrior kings like Edward III had excelled in the conquest of other nations. Englishmen are famous for their strength, their military successes, their masculinity. But to describe a category of men, however unimpeachably manly, as a 'breed', is to draw attention to the fact that somehow they must have been 'bred', and that therefore members of the female sex must have played in the process something more than a marginal role. Gaunt also talks about 'birth' (II.1.52), though he is there perhaps talking less about the biological process by which children are delivered than about the male-dominated dynastic system of lineage. More distinctively revealing are his references to England as a 'nurse' and as a 'teeming womb of royal kings' (II.1.51), metaphors which draw attention to the specifically female capacities of gestation and suckling. As Gaunt's celebration of the achievements of the English aristocracy extends to include the crusades, he actually finds space to mention a woman's name:

> . . . this teeming womb of royal kings,
> Feared by their breed, and famous by their birth,
> Renownèd for their deeds as far from home
> For Christian service and true chivalry
> As is the sepulchre in stubborn Jewry
> Of the world's ransom, blessèd Mary's son
>
> (II.1.51–56)

The allusion to the Virgin Mary is perhaps representative of Gaunt's view of women. Whatever cults of worship may attach to Mary, her primary significance is the fact that she gave birth to a remarkable man, Jesus. In Gaunt's feudal and aristocratic perspective, women appear as the passive vehicles by means of which the patriarchal seed is procreated, the patrilinear dynasty secured. Even the femininity of his metaphorical 'England' is ultimately spurious: since that maternal symbol is so completely a construction of the kings and warriors who have served their country in loyalty, fidelity and truth. Nonetheless, however, strenuous Gaunt's efforts to suppress the reality of the feminine, it continues to appear, if only in the interstices of his metaphorical language. You cannot really talk about nurses, and wombs, and birth, and breeding, without bringing into play a feminine dimension of meaning. Once that meaning occupies a space inside the imaginative universe of the play, it proves remarkably hard to expel.

We will now examine the part played in the drama by its three female characters. All three are present in the play not in their own right, or because they have any distinctive individual contribution to make to the play's action: but in terms of their relationships with men. They are all, primarily and even exclusively, wives and mothers. The Duchess of Gloucester is there to lament and preserve the memory of her murdered husband. The Duchess of York is there to plead, successfully, for the life of Aumerle her son. Queen Isabel has literally nothing to do in the play except to feel sadness and pity for her husband.

The Duchess of Gloucester seems to represent a potentiality for female assertiveness, which is nonetheless deflected and turned to self-destructive grief and melancholy. Her husband the Duke of Gloucester (Thomas of Woodstock) has been murdered (or summarily executed) by the King. In her view Gloucester's murder was a dreadful crime, since it was not only an unlawful killing, not only an offence committed against a kinsman (Gloucester was one of Richard's uncles), but a violation of the royal family itself. Where Richard sees royalty as inhering in his own person, the Duchess conceives of it as a shared possession dispersed across the family of Edward III, and rooted in each of his seven sons. In killing Gloucester, Richard has struck at the very root of the aristocratic kinship system itself.

The Duchess seeks to persuade Gaunt to take revenge against Richard; but Gaunt is committed to preserving the security of the crown, however much he may disapprove of the particular king who wears it. The Duchess's hopes of revenge focus therefore on the possibility of Bolingbroke's emerging victorious from the combat with Mowbray. If Bolingbroke were to kill Mowbray, then a kinsman of Gloucester's would have succeeded in killing his murderer, and in casting a guilty shadow over the instigator of the murder, Richard himself. Revenge would be satisfied, her dead husband's ghost appeased:

> O, sit my husband's wrongs on Hereford's spear
> That it may enter butcher Mowbray's breast!
> Or if misfortune miss the first career,
> Be Mowbray's sins so heavy in his bosom
> That they may break his foaming courser's back

And throw the rider headlong in the lists,
A caitiff recreant to my cousin Hereford.

(I.2.47–53)

Such militant violence of language proves the Duchess capable of that hot-blooded martial vigour defined by Mowbray as the peculiar prerogative of the male sex. But however strong her feelings, and however forceful their expression, this is still 'the trial of a woman's war': for the Duchess is prevented by the impotence of her gender from acting upon her impulses towards revenge and restitution. She can only ask men to act for her, or support their struggles from the sidelines like a superannuated cheerleader. Her energies frustrated by circumstances, they collapse back into the confused grief and melancholy which evidently kill her:

Desolate, desolate will I hence and die.
The last leave of thee takes my weeping eye.

(I.2.73–74)

That condition of melancholy seems to be the natural lot of women in this play. Our introduction to Queen Isabel is to a mood of unfocused sadness, a grief without cause, which yet proves to be a prophetic monitor of imminent calamity. Isabel naturally uses the imagery of pregnancy and birth, but displaces such possibilities from her own body, envisaging the birth of nothing but misfortune:

Some unborn sorrow ripe in fortune's womb
Is coming towards me . . .

II.2.10–11)

When Green brings the news of Bolingbroke's return from banishment, that phantom pregnancy is delivered of its burden of sorrow.

So, Green, thou art the midwife to my woe,
And Bolingbroke my sorrow's dismal heir.
Now hath my soul brought forth her prodigy,
And I, a gasping new-delivered mother,
Have woe to woe, sorrow to sorrow joined.

(II.2.62–66)

This imagery of perverted maternity is clearly there for a purpose, and can be connected with John of Gaunt's use of maternal imagery, discussed above. That great noble, who is also a notable father, a formidable patriarch (his son will become king), sees women as the passive and marginal bearers of masculine power: their job is to bear sons. Only in that capacity do they attain any real significance. The patriarchal ethic is thus somewhat hard on Queen Isabel, since circumstances will prevent her from fulfilling that function: she will not bear Richard's children. Deprived by fate of what is seen as the only kind of power women can possess, the power to reproduce men, Isabel's lot seems unspeakably and inconsolably sad. In place of the child she will not bear, the Gardener plants, in elegiac remembrance of her sorrow, a 'bank of rue':

> Rue even for ruth here shortly shall be seen
> In the remembrance of a weeping Queen.

> > (III.4.106–107)

In the Queen's last scene (V.1) where she takes leave of the deposed King, Isabel laments Richard's fall, and in doing so she acknowledges the blossom of her own life to be 'withered':

> But soft, but see, or rather do not see,
> My fair rose wither.

> > (V.1.7–8)

Again, her function is quite literally marginal: to stand by the roadside to observe the 'woeful pageant' of the King's disgrace. Here however Isabel makes her one display of strength, manifesting that potentiality for resistance already seen in the Duchess of York:

> The lion dying thrusteth forth his paw
> And wounds the earth, if nothing else with rage
> To be o'erpowered. And wilt thou pupil-like
> Take the correction, mildly kiss the rod . . .?

> > (V.1.29–32)

But whatever reserves of strength and defiance the woman has, she cannot act for herself: she can only ask men to act for her. Richard's reponse to this encouragement is to declare that he

is, in effect, already dead, and the Queen already ('Good sometimes queen' — V.l.37) a widow.

The play has only one more female character to offer us, the
Duchess of York: but hers is by contrast a success story. Her
importance is that she is mother to Aumerle, the young
associate of Richard's who becomes involved in a conspiracy to
assassinate Henry, and is detected by his father, York. She is
a mother: now too old to bear children, she cannot bear the
thought of losing her son, since such a loss would deprive her
of the significance of her existence, reduce her to the shadowy
unreality of childless Isabel:

> Is not my teeming-date drunk up with time?
> And wilt thou pluck my fair son from mine age?
> And rob me of a happy mother's name?

> (V.2.91–93)

In seeking to persuade York to protect his son, the Duchess
appeals to patriarchal ideology: Aumerle does not resemble her,
or any of her kin; he resembles only his father (lines 107–108).
York rides to the new king, and accuses his son of intended
treachery. The Duchess pleads for Aumerle to be pardoned, and
the pardon is granted by Henry. Mother and son unite successfully to oppose the will of the father: but only of course by
securing the intervention of a more powerful father-figure, the
King.

The play reveals quite clearly therefore that in this kind of
patriarchal society, dominated by powerful men and their
concerns, women have a purely marginal function. It cannot
convincingly be argued that the play simply presents that
condition as natural and unremarkable, since the women in the
play are the objects of a powerful sense of pity. Of course it is
easier to offer pity than to secure justice: and it could be argued
that Shakespeare's own ideology is as patriarchal as John of
Gaunt's, since the play cannot imagine women as anything
other than the instruments of men and the bearers and protec-
tors of male children. This is really the point where the debate
begins. My own conviction is that the play can be read as
demonstrative of a deep-seated structural injustice in the way
this society positions women: it provides them with only one
function, that of bearing sons, so that whether or not they

manifestly unrealised and unfulfilled. When Bushy attempts to comfort and console the Queen's nameless grief, he unwittingly discloses the strange and insubstantial existence allowed to women by this feudal and patriarchal society. In an elaborate conceit, Bushy argues that grief and sorrow multiply themselves into numerous 'shadows', so that when observed from an angle, like perspective paintings, they appear greater than their real substance. The Queen's sadness at her lord's departure is thus exaggerated into a disproportionate anxiety. But how then is the sufferer supposed to distinguish shadow from substance, reality from illusion? If Isabel looks correctly at the real conditions of her life, she will see 'naught but shadows/ Of what is not' (II.2.23–24). Thus we see the woman's life de-realised by the very pity that is offered as her consolation.

AFTERTHOUGHTS

1

What do you understand by the phrase 'unconscious misogyny' (page 57)?

2

What is the relevance to Holderness's argument of his reference to the Spanish Armada?

3

How far do you agree that Shakespeare intended to demonstrate 'a deep-seated structural injustice in the way this society positions women' (page 62)?

4

Compare Holderness's comments in this essay about the presentation of England in *Richard II* with the essays by Potter (pages 21–28) and by Devlin (pages 65–77).

Diana Devlin

Diana Devlin is a writer and teacher of Theatre Arts who has worked extensively in Britain and the USA. She is a director of the Shakespeare Globe Centre, a project to reconstruct Shakespeare's theatre on its original site.

ESSAY

'This earth, this realm, this England'

One of the most famous passages in Shakespeare is from John of Gaunt's prophecy about his country, spoken on his deathbed. These lines are frequently quoted in praise of England, but for anyone who knows their context, such use of them is strikingly inappropriate. Far from taking pride in his country, John of Gaunt is here lamenting its downfall under King Richard II. He paints a glorious picture only to tell his listeners how besmirched it is. The appropriate response is a contradictory one, pride and shame being equally mixed. The contradiction arises not only because of the sudden let-down two-thirds of the way through, but also because the preceding eulogy contains a series of images about England which do not themselves add up to a consistent meaning. One of the words put into Gaunt's mouth that is most rich in meaning, and most ambiguous, is 'earth'. Here, and in other parts of the play, Shakespeare draws out complex and sometimes contradictory meanings for 'earth' which affect the thought pattern of the whole play. By examining its significance in Gaunt's speech and in other parts of the play, we can see how Shakespeare creates meaning through images as well as through character and action. Nowadays, many metaphors are so well worn we cease to picture the images

C

on which they draw. (For example, in that last sentence the words 'worn' and 'draw' are both, strictly speaking, used metaphorically.) But in Shakespeare's writing we do well to see clearly in the mind's eye what he has imaged. Often it will conjure up a more vivid scene than the action taking place upon the stage.

Gaunt's description begins by identifying England with royalty:

> This royal throne of kings, this sceptred isle
>
> (II.1.40)

He thus makes the land itself the place where the king sits, a kind of giant throne-room. The following lines strengthen the image:

> This earth of majesty, this seat of Mars
>
> (II.1.41)

The earth has majesty *because* it is the seat of kings, and even of the god of war. This idea of kingship glorifying the country would seem to justify the self-aggrandisement we find in King Richard, since it is his kingship which enhances this earth. Yet only a few lines earlier Gaunt has insulted Richard, calling him an 'insatiate cormorant' which 'preys upon itself' (II.1.38, 39). There is a significant split in Gaunt's thought, dividing 'majesty' itself from the character of the King, and begging the question: where does the majesty of the earth come from, if not from the king himself?

The conflict between the ideal of kingship and the nature of the man who holds the office is one which fascinated Shakespeare; he dealt with it in many plays and never more fully than in *Richard II*, where Richard's sense of his kingship is so fatally at odds with his inadequacy at filling the role. Gaunt's speech sets out the contradiction and does not resolve it.

The next lines of the speech convey an equally elevated image of England, as another Garden of Eden:

> This other Eden — demi-paradise
>
> (II.1.42)

Here we are invited to see the country as directly blessed by God, without the need of kings or lesser gods. This is an alternative way of depicting England, rather than a development or resolution of the previous image. The implied image of a garden is not explored at this point, but Shakespeare returns to it much later in the play. In Act III, scene 4 two gardeners compare their work with that of the King and his government, calling England 'our sea-wallèd garden, the whole land' (III.4.43). This scene is one of the most extended, graphic similes in all Shakespeare's work, and since it too is about the image of England and of earth, it bears comparison with Gaunt's speech. The most important difference to note is that, while Gaunt's allusion to Eden suggests only God's beneficence, the Gardeners' dialogue emphasises the amount of human work that is necessary to keep a garden trim and flourishing.

Moving quickly on, Gaunt now develops another alternative image, based on England's strong natural defences, walled in by the sea:

> This fortress built by nature for herself
> Against infection and the hand of war,
> This happy breed of men, this little world,
> This precious stone set in the silver sea,
> Which serves it in the office of a wall,
> Or as a moat defensive to a house
> Against the envy of less happier lands
>
> (II.1.43–49)

These famous lines have always had a ringing force when there is a possibility of invasion from a force across the seas. (They laid the foundation for Winston Churchill's powerful rhetoric during the Second World War.) Certainly Richard's ability to defend himself against Bolingbroke's invasion was seriously weakened by his having left his 'fortress' to go to Ireland. But there are flaws in the 'island' image, given that England itself is not surrounded by the sea. The Welsh provided wavering help during this period, and Scotland was often hostile. Indeed, Bolingbroke himself was to fight the Scots during his own reign. More important for the development of imagery in the play is Gaunt's pride in 'this little world' and 'this precious stone set in the silver sea'. These images suggest a self-sufficiency and completeness that is at odds with his earlier attempt to console his son on being banished:

All places that the eye of heaven visits
Are to a wise man ports and happy havens.

(I.3.275–276)

Bolingbroke finds no comfort in those words, and Gaunt indeed admits that he is speaking out of necessity. Later we shall find that Mowbray, banished for life, did find fulfilment in another land.

Before continuing his image-building, Gaunt lists his definitions in the climactic line: 'This blessèd plot, this earth, this realm, this England' (II.1.50), but he still suspends the crucial verb which alone will reveal his intention in the speech. The repetition of the word 'earth', used earlier, is important because it makes the meaning both clearer and more confused. It arises naturally from 'this blessèd plot', as we visualise the plot of land and remember the Eden image, but 'earth' is also the opposite of 'heaven' and so the word carries the mind beyond England itself to signify the whole world, though that does not seem to have been Gaunt's intention since he links it so closely with the realm of England.

'Earth' is also the soil which nurtures growth. Perhaps it is this connotation which prompts Gaunt to another image of great importance in the play. From the idea of nurturing plants, earth may be imaged as a woman, nursing and begetting children, and so the earth of England becomes, in a new metaphor, 'This nurse, this teeming womb of royal kings' (II.1.51). The metaphor is new only to the speech, for Bolingbroke had already voiced it on banishment, addressing the earth as 'England's ground', as 'Sweet soil' and then as 'My mother and my nurse that bears me yet' (I.3.306, 307).

The personification of the English earth as a woman is in fact one of the most fruitful metaphors in the play. The Duke of York accuses Bolingbroke of marching across 'her peaceful bosom', and extends the image to include 'her pale-faced villages' (II.3.92, 93). While still confident of his own power, Richard reverses the child/mother relationship Bolingbroke and Gaunt had used, making himself more dominant than the earth:

Dear earth, I do salute thee with my hand,
Though rebels wound thee with their horses' hoofs.

> As a long-parted mother with her child
> Plays fondly with her tears and smiles in meeting,
> So weeping, smiling, greet I thee, my earth,
> And do thee favours with my royal hands.
>
> (III.2.6–11)

However, he quickly changes to a more supplicating form of address, asking 'my gentle earth' (III.2.12) to do annoyance to the rebels. It is indicative of Richard's character that, at this moment, he devotes himself to 11 lines of this 'senseless conjuration' (III.2.23) rather than deal with the matter in hand. One is also conscious of the possessive pronoun 'my', which he uses twice, perhaps emphasising that the earth is his, rather than that he is of the earth.

By this time in the play, the earth England has become virtually another character, having been physically greeted by Richard and had feelings ascribed to 'her'. 'She' is now to be fought over if necessary, like a damsel in a romance. Bolingbroke threatens 'a crimson tempest' (i.e. bloodshed), on 'The fresh green lap of fair King Richard's land' (III.3.46, 47). Richard retorts that that:

> Shall ill become the flower of England's face,
> Change the complexion of her maid-pale peace
> To scarlet indignation . . .
>
> (III.3.97–99)

After Bolingbroke's triumph, the Duchess of York transforms the woman image to signify the new times that are coming, enquiring with some sharpness:

> Who are the violets now
> That strew the green lap of the new-come spring?
>
> (V.2.46–47)

The final and remarkable development of the mother image is in the character of the Duchess herself, who comes like the incarnation of this pitiful 'earth' to plead to the new king, almost comically, for mercy and the restoration of peace in her family.

To return to Gaunt's great speech, his own image of the earth as mother and nurse is only fleeting, leading to praise for the chivalry and valour of her royal sons. However, in contrast to the earlier emphasis on England's shores, he extends their deeds well beyond them, alluding to the crusades to the Holy Land (II.1.53–56). So we have come full circle. Whereas, at the beginning, England was given majesty by being the seat of kings, now the chief claim is that this earth has herself brought forth kings who are famous for what they have done, not for England but for Christendom. At the time of the play, Christendom had been split by the Reformation, but Shakespeare projects the ideal of the Holy Crusades, still dear in Richard II's time.

We are now reaching the end of Gaunt's eulogy of England and can draw some conclusions. When the speech is taken completely out of context, it can be treated as a piece of patriotic rhetoric and has often been so anthologised. Taken in context, it is deeply ironic, a paeon of praise deliberately built up to a great climax, in order to make the anticlimax more effective, spoken by an experienced statesman well aware of the licence for free speech which the deathbed gives him. We have been looking at the idealised picture of England which Gaunt will now explode. However, it is clear that the picture itself is far from clear, for Gaunt leaves his main images unresolved. He sees the earth of England as a territory specially blessed by God and nature, another Eden, which, given its strong defences, might be expected to be self-sufficient under God. On the other hand, the second half of the eulogy sets up the chief virtue of this earth as producing kings who have left England to defend Christendom. This divided attitude to patriotism is dramatised later in the play through the different responses to banishment of Bolingbroke and Mowbray. The former returns to take possession of his lands, while the latter goes off and fights in the crusades. The Bishop of Carlisle's account of Mowbray contrasts with Gaunt's speech, suggesting that, unlike the main characters in the play, Mowbray was quite content to live and die on another part of the earth than England:

> Many a time hath banished Norfolk fought
> For Jesu Christ in glorious Christian field,
> Streaming the ensign of the Christian cross
> Against black pagans, Turks, and Saracens,

And, toiled with works of war, retired himself
To Italy, and there at Venice gave
His body to that pleasant country's earth

(IV.1.92–98)

Later we shall see that Bolingbroke too decides to go to the Holy Land, as the only way of washing off the blood he has caused to flow.

The turning point of Gaunt's speech is marked by the repetition of the word 'dear', playing on its two meanings of 'expensive' and 'cherished':

This land of such dear souls, this dear dear land,
Dear for her reputation through the world

(II.1.57–58)

At last, the long-awaited main verb of the sentence is spoken, given great significance by the delay, and clearly to be spoken weightily:

Is now leased out — I die pronouncing it —
Like to a tenement or pelting farm.

(lines 59–60)

The meaning is quite literal and practical. Richard, running short of money, has raised it on his lands and this shocks Gaunt. Later in the scene he tells Richard to his face, 'Landlord of England art thou now, not king' (line 113), and after Gaunt's death, Ross explains to the other discontented lords, 'The Earl of Wiltshire hath the realm in farm' (II.1.256).

The less of England that Richard owns, the less is he overall ruler and the less there can be a real identity between king and country. Richard has handed power to his favourites, who, in an image from the Gardeners' scene are the 'too fast-growing sprays/ That look too lofty in our commonwealth' (III.4.34–35). Gaunt is pinpointing a real loss of power, in contrast to the images of power of which he has spoken hitherto in the speech. In the next lines he plays on the possible double meaning of the word 'England', signifying both the country and the king, and also the two ways it is 'bound':

England, bound in with the triumphant sea,
Whose rocky shore beats back the envious siege

Of watery Neptune, is now bound in with shame,
With inky blots and rotten parchment bonds.

(II.1.61–64)

The sea is no longer 'silver' or 'a moat defensive' but 'triumphant' and besieging the shore which must beat it back; the
change in the image is linked to the shame of parcelling
England up in bonds. Gaunt's final judgement convinces us of
the scandal he feels it to be. It also links back to the earlier
image of Richard as the cormorant preying on itself:

That England that was wont to conquer others
Hath made a shameful conquest of itself.

(II.1.65–66)

Within a few moments of that death, Richard has snatched John
of Gaunt's lands away, depriving Bolingbroke of his inheritance
and provoking his return from banishment to claim it. He
abuses the very principle, inheritance, on which his power as
king is based. This is indicative of his own divided attitude to
'my earth', which he believes was granted him by divine right
and is unaffected by what use he makes of it.

We see then, in the final part of Gaunt's speech, an attitude
to the land of England which is defined, not by an ideal, but by
legal ownership. It may be difficult for us to identify with
Gaunt's anger, but Shakespeare's audience would have felt more
deeply the significant shift away from a medieval system of
fealty and allegiance to the king, towards a state of affairs
where property deals proliferated, and where division and sub-
division of lands led to a decrease in real concern for the land.
Gaunt's sense of shame arises from a disillusionment that was
perhaps inevitable for an old man. His ideal of England as a
'demi-paradise' is too unrealistic to bear examination. The
alternative ideal that Shakespeare sets up is that of the real
garden, contrasting Richard's careless stewardship of his kingdom
with that of the wise gardener (though Shakespeare's audience
might still have understood the gardener to connote Adam):

We at time of year
Do wound the bark, the skin of our fruit trees,
Lest being overproud in sap and blood
With too much riches it confound itself.

> Had he done so to great and growing men
> They might have lived to bear, and he to taste
> Their fruits of duty. Superfluous branches
> We lop away that bearing boughs may live.
> Had he done so, himself had borne the crown
> Which waste of idle hours hath quite thrown down.
>
> (III.4.57–66)

Other images and connotations of the earth occur in the play. One idea the Elizabethans would have associated with the earth was the division of the world into the four elements of earth, air, fire and water. The second, air, is not prominent in the play, although the word 'breath' is frequent. But King Richard is often likened to fire, as in Gaunt's 'blaze of riot' mentioned above, while Bolingbroke, in his raging advance on the land is likened to water:

> Like an unseasonable stormy day
> Which makes the silver rivers drown their shores
> As if the world were all dissolved to tears
>
> (III.2.106–108)

Although the fire/water images are often used without 'earth' being mentioned, the familiarity of the elements must have conjured up, for Shakespeare's audience, a picture of the earth over which Richard and Bolingbroke struggle.

Bolingbroke takes up the idea of war between the elements as he challenges Richard's power at Berkeley Castle:

> Methinks King Richard and myself should meet
> With no less terror than the elements
> Of fire and water when their thundering shock
> At meeting tears the cloudy cheeks of heaven.
> Be he the fire, I'll be the yielding water;
> The rage be his, while on the earth I rain
> My waters — on the earth, and not on him.
>
> (III.3.54–60)

However, the clear differentiation between the elements of water and fire is not constant through the play. When, at the beginning of the play, Richard speaks of Bolingbroke's and Mowbray's rage, he combines both elements together:

In rage, deaf as the sea, hasty as fire.

(I.1.19)

Later, Bolingbroke combines the images of fire and frost, snow
and 'fantastic heat' (I.3.294–299). This mingling of the elements
prepares for the eventual switch, when Richard relinquishes his
association with fire, even as he relinquishes the crown. He
imagines Bolingbroke and himself as two buckets in a well:

> The emptier ever dancing in the air,
> The other down, unseen, and full of water.
> That bucket down and full of tears am I,
> Drinking my griefs whilst you mount up on high.

(IV.1.185–188)

Then he wishes Bolingbroke 'many years of sunshine days' (line
220), and, finally, brings the images of snow and heat together,
as Bolingbroke had done:

> O that I were a mockery king of snow,
> Standing before the sun of Bolingbroke,
> To melt myself away in water-drops.

(lines 259–261)

The switch of Bolingbroke's element from water to fire, far
from assuring us of his triumph, sows the seeds of doubt about
his future. Taken together with the image of buckets going up
and down, filling and emptying in turn, it suggests that kings
can be changed. This very point is made in real terms by
Richard, who foresees Northumberland's rebellion and Henry
Bolingbroke's lasting distrust of him, since those who know how
to 'plant unrightful kings' (V.1.63) may do it again.

In following the fire/water/earth association to its
conclusion, I have anticipated the other important image which
is at first associated with Richard, and then transferred to
Bolingbroke. This is the image of the sun, the eye of heaven,
which is raised over the earth. This image is used most powerfully in the scene of Richard's return from Ireland. He describes
how, when the sun is absent, villains can go about their work
in the dark, undetected, but when it shines, it lights up their
wicked deeds (III.2.36–46). Then with characteristic pride, he
takes the sun image to himself:

So when this thief, this traitor Bolingbroke
. . .
Shall see us rising in our throne, the east,
His treasons will sit blushing in his face,
Not able to endure the sight of day,
But self-affrighted, tremble at his sin.

(III.2.47–53)

With this imagery, he sets himself on a level with heaven.
Clearly Richard himself is here the usurper, of heavenly not of
earthly power. His assertion of faith in the durability of his
divine kingship, which follows immediately, must surely be
taken as false pride and hyperbole, even though it confirms an
accepted Elizabethan belief:

Not all the water in the rough rude sea
Can wash the balm off from an anointed king.

(lines 54–55)

Richard's confidence that the angels are ready to fight for him
crumbles quickly in the face of real events. Later, he acknowledges his mistake, comparing himself with 'glistering Phaethon'
(III.3.178), who flew too near the sun. Richard clearly fails
against the ideal of the chivalric and crusading king fighting for
the sake of Christ, because he rates the kingly position nearer
to heaven than earth.

The question of righteous kingship is not resolved in the
play. Shakespeare would return to it in later plays. What the
images of 'earth' show us is that the ideal king must tend his
kingdom like a garden, and be aware that his righful place
during his life is on the earth and not in heaven. Richard fails
on these counts too, opening the way for Bolingbroke's usurpation. But taking the throne away from a rightful heir cannot
be justified, so Bolingbroke's deeds are seen as wrongful too. In
a speech that parallels John of Gaunt's against Richard, the
Bishop of Carlisle prophesies the unhappiness ahead if Bolingbroke becomes king, painting vivid images of the doomed earth:

The blood of English shall manure the ground,
And future ages groan for this foul act.
Peace shall go sleep with Turks and infidels,
And in this seat of peace tumultuous wars

Shall kin with kin, and kind with kind, confound.
Disorder, horror, fear, and mutiny
Shall here inhabit, and this land be called
The field of Golgotha and dead men's skulls.
O, if you raise this house against this house
It will the woefullest division prove
That ever fell upon this cursèd earth.

(IV.1.137–147)

There are few metaphors in this speech, but the images of England and its earth that have already enriched the play resonate through it here. The 'field of Golgotha' contrasts harshly with the 'other Eden', the sense of the earth as a wounded mother is felt without being worded. The most powerful metaphor is of the blood which will 'manure' the ground, giving a sharp and cruel change to the idea of earth as the source of growth. At the end of the play, Bolingbroke recognises that his guilt in Richard's death is against heaven. He seeks to blot it out with the only deed the play recognises as truly holy, and he expresses his intention in words that echo Carlisle's meaning:

Lords, I protest, my soul is full of woe
That blood should sprinkle me to make me grow.
. . .
I'll make a voyage to the Holy Land
To wash this blood off from my guilty hand.

(V.6.45–50)

However emotive the images of earth that the characters in the play have conjured up for their own purposes, there is one image of the earth that presents an incontrovertible truth — of mortality. Near the beginning, Mowbray speaks of man as 'gilded loam, or painted clay' without his reputation (I.1.178–179). Gaunt speaks of his grave as a 'hollow womb' (II.1.83); Richard faces the truth of his own condition most honestly when he admits, less than a hundred lines after his speech equating himself with the sun:

And nothing can we call our own but death
And that small model of the barren earth
Which serves as paste and cover to our bones.

(III.2.152–154)

This brief examination of the images and associations of the word 'earth' cannot cover all the examples in the play. It has perhaps shown the meanings on which the play pivots, rather than the emotional force the word 'earth' exerts on almost every character, whether he/she sees it as the land of their birth, as the sphere of mortal life, as the soil on which bloodshed might flow, or as the dust to which we all return. As we have seen from John of Gaunt's speech, meanings flow in and out of each other, with metaphorical and concrete images mingling. In this context, Richard's reliance on words rather than deeds as the source of his power becomes understandable. Lastly, the abundance of 'earth' images (which may indeed hinder the characters from keeping 'their feet on the ground'!) derives from Shakespeare's understanding of natural earth. Rain, sun, the seasons, growth, overgrowth and decay, whatever plays a part in earth's cycle, Shakespeare draws into the tapestry of England he creates in this play.

AFTERTHOUGHTS

1

How does Devlin develop her argument that the first two-thirds of John of Gaunt's speech contains 'a series of images about England which do not themselves add up to a consistent meaning' (page 65)?

2

What distinction does Devlin draw here between the garden image in John of Gaunt's speech and the imagery in the later garden scene?

3

What examples of 'images and associations of the word "earth"' (page 77) are highlighted in this essay? In what ways do they enrich the play's meaning?

4

Compare Devlin's comments in this essay about the presentation of England in *Richard II* with the essays by Potter (pages 21–28) and by Holderness (pages 53–63).

Ronald Draper

*Ronald Draper is Regius Professor of
Literature at the University of Aberdeen,
and the author or numerous scholarly
publications.*

ESSAY

'I wasted time, and now doth time waste me'

In his last great soliloquy before his murder in the Castle of
Pomfret Richard II debates with himself the tragic irony and
pathos of his situation as a king and no king, one who has
enjoyed the greatest power accorded to man on earth and yet
now sees himself reduced to nothingness. 'I wasted time,' he
reflects, 'and now doth time waste me' (V.5.49). The figure of
speech is typically rhetorical. Its technical name is *antimetabole*
a 'cross' figure in which words are repeated in inverse order:
ABBA — in this instance 'waste' and 'time', followed by 'time'
and 'waste'. There is also a third element of repetition in the
form of the first person singular which is a little less obvious
because of the change from 'I' (subject) to 'me' (object); but this
is, if anything, even more important since it highlights
Richard's change of role from active agent, 'I', to passive sufferer
of action, 'me'. The placing of 'I' at the beginning of the line and
'me' at the end further emphasises this change of role: the man
who starts by being in command, ends by being commanded.

This line and its rhetorical patterning sum up the career of
Richard as Shakespeare presents it in his play. In the first half
he is a hereditary monarch who can trace his lineage through
uninterrupted succession back to William the Conqueror, but

who throws away the power and prestige which this confers upon him; in the second half he is stripped of his titles and becomes belatedly aware of the extent to which his own mismanagement has contributed to his downfall. He 'wastes time' in that he both fails to take advantage of his great opportunities and imports disorder into a situation which calls for orderly conduct and the rule of law; and 'time wastes' him by both punishing him for his offence against order in not conducting himself as a rightful monarch should, and exposing him to the opportunism of Bolingbroke, who takes the chance, when it is offered him, to seize power and establish himself as king, if not by right, then at least by might. His very failure to act positively boomerangs on Richard and causes him to become the victim of his own inactive fecklessness; wasting leads to being wasted, and the King who should be the dominant 'I' becomes the subjugated 'me'.

Behind all this lies a complex sense of what kingship is and what possession of the royal office entails. The traditional view, embodied — to use E M W Tillyard's convenient phrase — in 'the Elizabethan world picture', places the king at the head of an elaborate social hierarchy which reaches down through the aristocracy, the clerisy, and the commercial classes to the ordinary, unlettered peasant. This view emphasises the overriding duty of obedience to one's superiors. Each rank must obey the one above it; disturbance of the carefully interlocking structure of society is a most heinous offence, since the pattern is not merely man-made, but ordained by God. It corresponds to the divine plan for a perfectly ordered universe (though this has been disrupted by the fall of Adam and Eve from paradise, which brought sin and corruption into the creation), and is reflected, and reinforced, by the corresponding hierarchies which exist in the physical world and the parallel structures of the animal kingdom. Thus the sun is the 'king' of the universe and the planets are hierarchically subordinate to it, and the lion is the 'king' of beasts, with gradations of animal beings beneath him which correspond to those beneath the human monarch. The classic exposition of this view is to be found in Ulysses's speech to the Greek warriors in *Troilus and Cressida*, where he attributes their failure in the siege of Troy to the dissension within their own army. When rank and authority are not respected, he argues, crippling disorder follows, spreading until it involves the entire universe in catastrophic chaos:

> Take but degree away, untune that string,
> And hark what discord follows! Each thing melts
> In mere oppugnancy: the bounded waters
> Should lift their bosoms higher than the shores,
> And make a sop of all this solid globe,
> Strength should be lord of imbecility,
> And the rude son should strike his father dead;
> Force should be right; or, rather, right and wrong —
> Between whose endless jar justice resides —
> Should lose their names, and so should justice too.
>
> (*Troilus and Cressida*, I.3.109–118)

In *Richard II* the chief exponent of this traditional view is the Bishop of Carlisle, and, appropriately, his most powerful expression of it comes at the point in Act IV when Bolingbroke, the usurper, declares that 'In God's name' he will 'ascend the regal throne' (line 113). The Bishop's deepest principles are outraged by Bolingbroke's use of the divine formula; his shocked reaction is, 'Marry, God forbid!', and he goes on to outline the terrible consequences which will result if Richard's deposition takes place:

> The blood of English shall manure the ground,
> And future ages groan for this foul act.
> Peace shall go sleep with Turks and infidels,
> And in this seat of peace tumultuous wars
> Shall kin with kin, and kind with kind, confound.
> Disorder, horror, fear, and mutiny
> Shall here inhabit, and this land be called
> The field of Golgotha and dead men's skulls.
>
> (IV.1.137–144)

The civil war implied in line 141 does, in fact, break out subsequently. Bolingbroke has scarcely become Henry IV before he finds himself faced with the conspiracy of Aumerle, the Abbot of Westminster, the Bishop of Carlisle, Salisbury, Spencer, Blunt, Kent, Brocas and Seely, and some of his chief supporters, including Northumberland, Worcester and Percy, are in rebellion against him soon after the opening of the next play, *Henry*

IV, Part 1. In *Henry VI, Part 3* (which had already been written and produced prior to *Richard II*, though it deals with the reign of a king who comes at a later historical period than Richard) the words 'kin with kin, and kind with kind, confound' are given dramatic embodiment in a scene which contains the graphic stage direction: 'Enter a Son that hath killed his Father, at one door; and a Father that hath killed his Son, at another door' (II.5.54). Thus Carlisle's prophecies not only have the support of orthodox Elizabethan doctrine, but are shown as coming true both within the bounds of this play and in Shakespeare's other history plays as well.

Such reinforcement, it might be argued — and has, indeed, been argued by commentators who emphasise Shakespeare's adherence to the 'degree' system — shows quite clearly where the sympathies of the dramatist lie. The king stands for legitimacy, and his deposition is an overthrow of divinely sanctioned order which has the direst consequences imaginable. Richard himself elaborates in the grandest manner on his kingly status, comparing himself, in the language of the order pattern, to the sun, and proclaiming his sacred imprint indelible:

> Not all the water in the rough rude sea
> Can wash the balm off from an anointed king.
> The breath of worldly men cannot depose
> The deputy elected by the Lord

> (III.2.54–57)

And in the following scene he insists on the appalling nature of the divine retribution which will be visited on his rebellious subjects:

> . . . God omnipotent,
> Is mustering in his clouds on our behalf
> Armies of pestilence; and they shall strike
> Your children yet unborn and unbegot,
> That lift your vassal hands against my head
> And threat the glory of my precious crown.

> (III.3.85–90)

However, like the Player-Queen in *Hamlet*, it seems Richard doth protest too much. Already in III.2 he has shown a capacity for exaggeration which makes his position suspect. His faith in

God's backing becomes overweening confidence when he declares egregiously that for every man conscripted by Bolingbroke, 'God for his Richard hath in heavenly pay/ A glorious angel' (III.2.60–61); and he reaches the point of absurdity when he asks the rhetorical question, 'Is not the King's name twenty thousand names?' — capping it with the fatuous battle cry: 'Arm, arm, my name! A puny subject strikes/ At thy great glory' (lines 85–87).

Such extravagance betrays the extent to which doctrine has become an unrealistic obsession with Richard. Whatever truth there might be, to Elizabethan ears at any rate, in the claim that 'divinity doth hedge a king' (to use another famous phrase from *Hamlet*), Richard's apparent willingness to ignore the crucial distinction between the symbolic significance of a 'name' and the facts of military strength reveals the inherent brittleness of his purely theoretical position. In this same scene the Bishop of Carlisle — eloquent spokesman for kingship though he is — presents a more sensible view which recognises the realities of 'power' as well as the prestige of kingly title, arguing, in effect, that God helps those who help themselves — or, at least, those who do not refuse 'The proffered means of succour and redress' (lines 27–32); and Aumerle rubs in the lesson more bluntly when he interprets the Bishop as meaning 'that we are too remiss,/ Whilst Bolingbroke through our security [=overconfidence]/ Grows strong and great in substance and in power' (lines 33–35).

But Richard is incapable of achieving a balanced view; he swings from one extreme to the other. His instantaneous resort to doctrinal fantasy masks a self-doubt which just as quickly, and immoderately, reveals itself in a disturbing switchback of alternating attitudes, from excessive assurance to premature despair. One piece of bad news from Salisbury and he is ready to capitulate:

> All souls that will be safe fly from my side,
> For time hath set a blot upon my pride.

(lines 80–81)

Aumerle's attempt to correct this, 'Remember who you are', causes him to veer the other way, but then Scroop's account of the deaths of Bushy, Green and Wiltshire plunges him back again into self-indulgent brooding on the mortuary themes 'of graves, of worms, and epitaphs' (line 145 etc.). His friends remind him of the need for action, and his 'ague-fit' is 'over-blown'; difficulties are minimised: 'An easy task it is to win our own' (lines 190–191). But news of York's desertion punctures him yet again, and he then resentfully rejects comfort of any kind whatever:

> By heaven, I'll hate him everlastingly
> That bids me be of comfort any more.

(lines 207–208)

The whole scene is thus one of vacillation revealing Richard's temperamental volatility and his total inability to make an effective connection between the symbolic world of kingship doctrine and the political realities of the world in which he must exercise kingly power.

Nevertheless, this scene is marked by a developing serious-ness and gravity of tone which contrasts with the different kind of irresponsibility, and even frivolity, of the scenes prior to Bolingbroke's return from banishment. At the beginning of the play Richard is faced with the confrontation between Mowbray and Bolingbroke. Because of its sinister political overtones this is a problem which needs to be handled both firmly and circum-spectly, especially in view of his own obscure involvement in the subject of the quarrel — the death of his uncle, Gloucester. Richard, however, treats the occasion as one for theatrical display. When he calls the two men into his presence it is with evident relish for the histrionic opposition to be expected:

> Face to face,
> And frowning brow to brow, ourselves will hear
> The accuser and the accusèd freely speak.
> High-stomached are they both, and full of ire;
> In rage, deaf as the sea, hasty as fire.

(I.1.15–19)

Conscious as he is that one of the contestants, Bolingbroke, is his own cousin, son of his principal counsellor, his uncle, John of Gaunt, he nonetheless makes a deliberate parade of impar-tiality; and though giving each man full scope to work himself up to a pitch of angry defiance, culminating in the challenge to

trial by combat, he poses as a peace-maker, urging them to
'Forget, forgive, conclude, and be agreed' — only to undercut the
solemnity of his chosen role with an ill-judged witticism: 'Our
doctors say this is no month to bleed' (lines 156–157). Then,
persuasion having failed, he resorts to command, telling Gaunt
to order Bolingbroke to throw down Mowbray's gage, and
himself ordering Mowbray to throw down Bolingbroke's. 'Lions
make leopards tame' (line 174), asserts Richard; but neither
obeys, whereupon he makes a show of turning the conflict into
a characteristically medieval contest of 'chivalry' (line 203). In
I.3 this is staged magnificently, with much sounding of trum-
pets, elaborate costumes (each man enters 'knightly-clad in
arms' (line 12)) and a profusion of rhetorical devices as formal
announcement is made of the contestants' titles. Their grounds
of complaint are then rehearsed, and with much ceremony each
makes a highly sentimental farewell. On the very brink of
actual combat, however, Richard suspends the lists by melo-
dramatically throwing down his warder. He consults with his
advisers, and decides that, after all, peace-making must be his
role — which represents true kingly motivation, expressed in
terms that show proper consideration for his realm ('for our eyes
do hate the dire aspect/ Of civil wounds ploughed up with neigh-
bours' sword' — lines 127–128), but devalued here by Richard's
vacillation. Bloodshed is therefore replaced by sentences of
banishment; but, finally, despite his earlier boast of impar-
tiality, he banishes Mowbray for life and Bolingbroke for ten
years, and compounds this impression of arbitrariness still
further by reducing his cousin's exile to six.

   In I.4 the King's frivolity is made still more apparent as he
allows himself, and his circle of favourites, to scoff at Bolingbroke's banishment (as well as revealing his jealousy of
Bolingbroke's popularity) and makes light of the exploitation of
his kingdom in order to pay for a punitive expedition to Ireland.
News that John of Gaunt is sick merely prompts him to
flippancy:

> Now put it, God, in the physician's mind
> To help him to his grave immediately!

(lines 59–60)

and this is carried over into II.1, where he visits his uncle and

the curious idea of the crown as a place where Death keeps its court, and having once seized on this theme he teases out its possibilities in a series of fantastic images:

> . . . within the hollow crown
> That rounds the mortal temples of a king
> Keeps death his court; and there the antic sits,
> Scoffing his state and grinning at his pomp,
> Allowing him a breath, a little scene,
> To monarchize, be feared, and kill with looks,
> Infusing him with self and vain conceit,
> As if this flesh which walls about our life
> Were brass impregnable; and humoured thus,
> Comes at the last, and with a little pin
> Bores through his castle wall, and — farewell king!
>
> (III.2.160–170)

Richard creates a little verbal play-within-the-play, based on the medieval *danse macabre* in which personified death leads men and women a dance around, and finally into, their own graves. Death has already been shown at work in this play with the death of John of Gaunt, but Richard then seemed insensitive to its reality. Now he is keenly conscious of its power to undermine human vanity and with a puny 'pin' reduce a monarch's self-esteem to nothingness. The splendour of his 'name', on which elsewhere he expends so much verbal energy, is thus provided with a very different context, and he, at least momentarily, pierces through the façade of kingship to the common condition of mortality which lies beneath it. Indeed, Richard invites his hearers to 'throw away respect,/ Tradition, form, and ceremonious duty', and speaks of himself as a commoner sharing the same vulnerable humanity as themselves:

> I live with bread, like you; feel want,
> Taste grief, need friends.
>
> (lines 175–176)

It is as if in the process of exploring his imaginative idea he anticipates the tragic lessons learnt by Lear and Gloucester in *King Lear*. It is obvious, of course, that he doesn't actually do so. For Richard this is merely word-spinning; he has not yet learnt what it really is to be reduced by bitter experience to the knowledge of his own participation in the universal human condition. But his words nonetheless open up vistas of tragic possibility and their effect, though ambiguous, is to make Richard seem a more complex and compelling figure.

The conflicting comments made by other characters in the play likewise add to this more complicated view of Richard. For example, the Duke of York, whose divided loyalties (Bolingbroke's demand to have his father's inheritance restored seems a reasonable one to him) and realistic appreciation of the political situation lead him to change sides, can still insist, in III.3, that Richard looks 'like a king' (line 68). Likewise, in the somewhat allegorical scene which follows, the Gardener's description of Richard as 'the wasteful King' who has brought disaster on his realm and himself by failing to cultivate and prune the garden of England harks back to earlier adverse comments; but the compassion and indignation aroused in Queen Isabel has the effect of enlisting sympathy for Richard, while her religious language ('What Eve, what serpent hath suggested thee/ To make a second Fall of cursèd man?' — III.4.75–76) paves the way for Richard's self-imaging as a Christ-figure whose deposition is an act of the gravest sacrilege.

The combined effect of these various views of Richard is to make the audience increasingly aware of a situation which cannot be interpreted on one level only. The ground is prepared for his deposition so that when it does happen it is recognised as to a large extent inevitable; and Bolingbroke's opportunistic seizure of power is seen to represent precisely that capacity for shrewd appraisal of actual circumstance which Richard signally lacks. On the other hand, Richard's preoccupation with the theme of kingship makes it impossible to ignore the illicit nature of his usurpation, and tacitly reminds us that Bolingbroke is, after all, merely a clever manipulator of men and public opinion. Likewise, if Bolingbroke's laconic use of words combined with forcefulness in action contrasts favourably with Richard's verbosity, such prosaic virtues also suggest lack of imagination; and if the corollary for Richard is over-abundance of imagination, running to verbal ingenuity and histrionic self-indulgence, these are qualities which also seem inseparable from the exploratory, and at least potentially tragic, power of his language. Richard in adversity thus becomes a tantalising figure. He seems to be at once deepening his awareness of his essential humanity and at the same time continuing his old frivolity of mind (though, as already indicated, with far greater linguistic inventiveness). This is never more apparent than in the climactic scene of the deposition itself (IV.1). There he makes a highly theatrical game of his own uncrowning, bringing together both verbal conceit and stage performance as he invites Bolingbroke to hold one side of the crown, while he himself holds the other, and proceeds to elaborate his image of the two buckets 'filling one another' (lines 180ff). The ritualistic language of parallelism and repetition in which he formally 'undoes himself' (lines 200–220) is a superb example of rhetorical exhibitionism, and his image of himself as 'a mockery king of snow' melting 'before the sun of Bolingbroke' (lines 259–261) is a consummately executed figure of pathos. But more serious depths are touched as well. The intricate punning of his reply to Bolingbroke's question whether he is willing to abdicate: 'Ay, no. No, ay; for I must nothing be' (line 200), is a mixture of paradoxical play and shrewd insight. At one level it expresses that *antimetabole* of vacillation — conceding, denying; denying, conceding again — which has been such a striking feature of his previous conduct, while at another it suggests his dawning awareness of the essentially contradictory nature of his situation. To answer 'yes' would be to negate that 'I' which has hitherto been inextricably involved with its own royal status — that is, to dissolve his being into nothingness. A single word would bring about its own opposite. And yet Richard is simultaneously aware that it is not within his power to withhold the word of assent. 'Therefore', he continues, his reply must be 'no no, for I resign to thee' — a double negative which conveys both horrified rejection (No! No!) and recognition that Bolingbroke will not take 'no' for an answer. Later he offers a further variation on such self-contradiction in his reluctance to read the articles listing the misdemeanors which have brought this disgrace upon him; his eyes are 'full of tears', he says, so that he cannot see, and yet he is not so blind but that he 'can see a sort of traitors here' (lines 243–245). His accusation is directed outward against his foes, but he also perceives his own treachery against himself in that he has paradoxically consented to 'undeck the pompous body of a king' and has 'Made glory base, and sovereignty a slave;/ Proud majesty, a subject; state, a peasant' (lines 246–251). The element of verbal play still obscures the extent to which this is true tragic recognition; but with the further histrionic business of the smashing of the looking-glass (line 275 etc.) Richard makes a deliberate analysis of his own image, or 'face', as it is presented to the outside world, which culminates in his enunciation of the more significant truth that all these examples of play-acting and verbal elaboration are 'merely shadows to the unseen grief/ That swells with silence in the tortured soul' (lines 296–297).

In these words the King who has hitherto seemed to be primarily a king of verbal gestures points to a language of silence which is beyond words. He does not, it is true, thereupon cease to be a player with words, but he does seem to touch the verge of a recognition that kingship, even in its most refined sense, is a matter of highly sophisticated posturing. By the very process of playing his regal role up to the hilt he comes to realise that it is indeed nothing but a role — a brittle human device, bolstered by doctrinal authority, but not substantial in itself. While the paraphernalia of 'degree' can be maintained, its psychological effect may be relatively potent, but once that mystique is penetrated it is seen to have no absolute reality. The only true absolute is the 'nothing' which is revealed when the King is stripped of his titles and finds himself reduced to his inherent weakness as a fallible, mortal human being.

This is perhaps what Richard finally grasps in the soliloquy which precedes his death in V.5. And with this realisation comes the guilty acceptance that as a kingly play-actor and verbal embellisher he has been culpably negligent in allowing himself to be deluded by the trappings of his office into behaving as if the office, irrespective of the behaviour of the office-bearer, were enough to secure his power. It is significant in this connection that his final gesture in killing two of his murderers before being struck down by Exton is his first real action, and that for the first time action now becomes associated with language which is plain and curt, without the cynical flippancy of his earlier days. For once Richard responds to a situation with complete commitment. He is here neither the exploiter of his 'name', nor the passive witness to his own regal dismemberment. His resistance is, of course, futile in that it cannot prevent his murder, but the fact that he neither resigns himself to his end fatalistically, nor allows his death to become a scene of introspectively adorned pathos, does hint at some closing of the gap in his previously divided personality.

As we have seen, it is also just prior to this moment that Richard pronounces the self-criticism quoted at the beginning of this essay: 'I wasted time, and now doth time waste me,' and in so doing he succeeds at last in seeing his career for what it has truly been. The killing of his attackers may not represent the achievement of a real ability to combine action and words in effectively kingly fashion (and if it did, his achievement would still have to be reckoned as too late to alter his fortunes), but it suggests that he has perhaps learnt something of the lesson of experience. Although his fate remains on balance pathetic rather than tragic, it is this deepening of introspection to the point where it emerges in a new and firmer quality of action that entitles him to be regarded as at least a potentially tragic figure. His final dying words pronounce a curse on Exton for staining the King's land with the King's blood and express a somewhat conventional idea of death as the separation of 'soul' and 'flesh' (V.5.109–112), but his moment of greatest insight is contained in his recognition of the way he has made a 'waste' of his temporal status and opportunities — followed by that tantalising glimpse of how things might have become different.

AFTERTHOUGHTS

1

How helpful do you find Draper's analysis of the 'rhetorical patterning' of the title quotation?

2

Compare the discussion of kingship in this essay with the essay by Selden (pages 104–111).

3

Explain the importance to Draper's argument of his interpretation of the 'hollow crown' speech (pages 88–89).

4

Do you agree that Richard's fate 'remains on balance pathetic rather than tragic' (page 92)?

Charles Moseley

*Charles Moseley teaches English at
Cambridge University and at the Leys
School, Cambridge. He is the author of
numerous critical studies.*

ESSAY

'This blessed plot': the garden scene in *Richard II*

Shakespeare wrote four plays dealing with the consequences of
the fall of Richard II: *Richard II, 1* and *2 Henry IV*, and *Henry
V*. Though they may not have been planned as a sequence, they
are closely linked in ideas, in symbols, and in imagery. At the
beginning of *1 Henry IV*, a striking image looks back to the
strife of *Richard II* and ironically forward to what is to come:

> No more the thirsty entrance of this soil
> Shall daub her lips with her own children's blood
>
> (I.1.5–6)

A mother greedily eating her own children is fit dominating
image for a play following on from the casual carnage of the best
blood in England that marked Henry's accession (*Richard II,*
V.6) and including within itself the death or execution of so
many nobles and commons. This grotesque, pointedly unnatural,
image of the mother eating her own children — the body politic

gone cannibal — continues, however, with a shift to another important idea:

> No more shall trenching war channel her fields,
> Nor bruise her flowerets with the armèd hoofs
> Of hostile paces.

(I.1.7–9)

We are now talking about gardens, husbandry and agriculture. Shakespeare has linked up the basic idea of the Motherland/Body Politic with the central theme, of the Garden and how it must be cultivated, which runs through all four plays. We moderns have virtually forgotten the symbolic power of gardens. Before we can understand Renaissance images and symbols of them we have to try to recover their original symbolic force. The idea of a garden needing tending runs through all the plays; in *Richard II* the scene (III.4) where the Queen and her ladies overhear the Gardeners talking is of central importance, setting up a controlling metaphor not only for the rest of that play but for the entire tetralogy. (The incident is quite unhistorical: Shakespeare's deliberate creation of it shows the importance he attached to it.) If we are to get anywhere near the force of this particular scene, we need to be clear where Shakespeare's major interests lie in these four histories, and we also need to try to feel as best we can something of that Renaissance fascination for the art of gardening as an analogy of the management of the little kingdom, Man, the greater kingdom, the State, and the government of the whole Universe.

Shakespeare's history plays are no facile celebration of the virtues of a God-given Tudor monarchy, ending the civil strife that stretched from the fall of Richard II in 1399 to the defeat of Richard III in 1485. Shakespeare in this group of plays examines the very nature of rule and of political relationships in the body politic. He is in no simple way examining how people are bound by the past in which they had no part. In a time of great perplexity and not a little fear, the examination, be it in the private reading of history or the public examination through the shared experience of history plays, of the body politic's distempers in the past might well seem to lead to a better understanding of those in the present — even, perhaps, a way of coping with them. For the contemporary relevance of Shakespeare's use of English history as myth cannot be too strongly stressed. The remark of Elizabeth, late in the decade in which *Richard II* was written, to William Lambarde when he described his researches in English history to her is often quoted: 'I am Richard II, know ye not that?' She lived in fear of her own Bolingbroke.

History began in a garden. According to the book of Genesis, God planted a garden east in Eden and gave it to man to look after. That 'happy garden state', where man 'knew not the doctrine of ill-doing', remained a potent image of perfection for literally thousands of years. It was, naturally, elaborated: the change of seasons and their accompanying discomfort was unknown, the plants gave their fruits in due time, the lion lay down with the lamb. But man's desire (or, to use the old and more correct term, his *cupiditas* — selfish desire as opposed to real love, self-giving and self-forgetting *caritas* — St Paul's 'charity' of 1 Corinthians 13) led him to seek a role and power that God had not given him, and so he fell. That Fall affected everything: man, the vital link in the chain of being, had failed, and everything below the broken link shared in its fall. Driven out of the garden, man was condemned to eat his bread in the sweat of his brow (Genesis 3) — in other words, work became the norm of his existence, and the failed gardener became a farmer. This notion of farming as the *best* fallen man can do is an important idea in Shakespeare's tetralogy.

The biblical idea of a state of original perfection, then ruined by man's action, was supported by classical sources too — for example Ovid and Virgil. Both strands affect deeply the medieval and Renaissance idea of the garden. In literature or in painting the garden can be a symbol of all possible virtue and delight, precarious or not; the design of real gardens in the fallen world can only glance obliquely at the ideal thing to which they refer, but even there the symbolism operates, and in the formal Renaissance garden with its complex mathematics and patterns there is an attempt to evoke something of the perfection of Eden. Discussion of gardening and planting could be more than just a primitive sort of Gardeners' Question Time: it was often serious debate about the role of fallen man in fallen nature, and there is a central moral and philosophical interest in the planting of knot-gardens or, later, of apparently 'natural' clumps of trees. We need to be very much on our guard, there-fore, as soon as we stray near a Renaissance flower bed, in art or on the ground, for one of the chief flowers in it is a symbolism of ideal perfection.

Man's primal sin changed the world for all time, and as these plays make despairingly clear, there is no undoing what once has been done. But God in his mercy gave man work to do, so that from the ruins of his original destiny he could painstak-ingly build something of real value. Law and hierarchy — rule — were, according to the theologians, instituted by the mercy of God to temper the effects of the Fall — as St Augustine put it, *in remedium peccatorum* — 'for the healing of sinners'. King-ship in general, therefore, in medieval and Renaissance thought, is frequently seen as serving a healing purpose in ruling: limiting the effects of man's sin by law and justice. It is against such a concept of kingship — where the king, fallen man himself though he be, should be the gardener of his realm, shepherd of his people and the voice of law embodied — that Shakespeare and his contemporaries ask us to judge their portrayals of indi-vidual kings.

The garden scene opens with the Queen asking two ladies how she shall 'drive away the heavy thought of care' in this garden — a remark that reminds us, if we needed it, that this likeness of Eden is only a distant echo. She rejects all four suggestions of amusement that are made: pleasure, even in those arts of music and dance whose order and pattern remind man of the harmony of the heavens above him, is beyond her troubled mind.

She draws aside with her ladies to observe the conversation of the Gardener and two servants, expecting them to 'talk of state' (line 27). There is a nice double irony here. In the conven-tion of pastoral poetry, use of which stretches from antiquity to the end of the eighteenth century, countryfolk frequently are made to discuss major moral and political issues: despite their humble station, they see more truly than great ones. The Queen is expecting the workmen to behave like characters in a pastoral she can comfortably observe. But because of the setting of the scene, she herself is *within* a pastoral, which here is explicitly a symbolic interpretation of Richard's conduct and situation.

Shakespeare has stressed the importance of what the Queen

D

overhears by breaking with the normal dramatic convention whereby rustics would speak in prose. This gardener and his mate speak in a blank verse that emphasises the seriousness and importance of what they have to say. The Gardener, as a good gardener should, is making proper use of his subordinate to look after his charge; to support the plants that need supporting, to prune the rank growth and uproot the weeds that harm the good plants. His imagery — 'unruly children' (line 30), 'executioner' (line 33), 'commonwealth' (line 35), 'government' (line 36) underlines the parallel between his role and that of a ruler. His man makes the parallel — 'model' (line 42) — come very near home; the terms and images of Gaunt's great protest about Richard's misgovernment in II.1 are newly focused in his words, for England is the 'sea-wallèd garden' (line 43), whose gardener has criminally shirked his duty. This makes those who have lesser gardens to cultivate question why they should do so. Richard's folly weakens the order that produces the very food on which men live. The extended image of the overgrown knot-garden, unweeded, unpruned, the useful plants 'Swarming with caterpillars' (line 47) cannot but remind us of Bolingbroke's image for Bushy, Green and Bagot, 'The caterpillars of the commonwealth' (II.3.165), and ironically of his momentary vision of himself as a gardener 'weed[ing] and pluck[ing them] away' (II.3.166). Those caterpillars are both symptom and effect of the mess England is in, the result of Richard's 'waste of idle hours' (III.4.66; cf. line 55).[1]

The abruptness of the Gardener's response shows a control, which Richard never showed, over a subordinate, whose toying with the idea of rebelliousness — getting above his station — must be nipped in the bud. His image of Richard as a great tree coming to the 'fall of leaf' (line 49) emphasises both the paradox of his sheltering what, like ivy, would ultimately destroy him, and through the imagery of the good management of a garden, the justice of what Bolingbroke has done (lines 51ff). Embodiment of law and majesty though Richard may be, he is still

---

[1] 'Waste' is a much more powerful word than it might seem: it then meant the evil misuse or misdirection of the goods of a state. (Much medieval satire is directed against 'wasters'. Bushy, Green and Bagot are, in Shakespeare's and his forefathers' terms 'wasters'.

subject to justice himself — and the more vulnerable as his responsibilities are greater. His mighty tree, it is implied, will itself be uprooted (lines 68–69). There is surely an echo in these lines, and in the image of tree-management in lines 57ff, of Jesus's warning that 'Every tree that bringeth not forth good fruit shall be plucked up and cast into the fire' (Matthew 3:10). In these lines (to line 66) the imagery of good and, by implication, bad husbandry is sustained in an elaborate conceit, which explores in considerable *and memorable* detail the duties of a king. Crucially, the image integrates the misconduct and what it deserved with the pathos of Richard's fall. The conceit hammers itself into our consciousness as a potent way of valuing and understanding the fall of Richard and *why* it has inevitably happened. The Gardener's lines, too, are not only an admonition in a play, not only of general relevance; they shoot straight out of the play and challenge the mighty of Shakespeare's own day to defend their stewardship.

The ideas of kingship so memorably stated here clearly have to be borne in mind when we look later at the reigns of Henry IV and Henry V. For this discussion relates closely to the contemporary ideas of the monarch's 'Two Bodies': the Prince is both mortal man, with the moral duties and obligations that no individual can escape, and also the mortal symbol of immortal Kingship, the embodiment of law and majesty and of the identity of the nation.

It is easy, when reading, to forget the Queen and her ladies. But in the theatre, she is visible, watching and hearing all this. We are watching her watching, and as we recognise the justice of the Gardener's extended analogy, we are also aware of its effect on her. For though the Gardener knows more than she does about Richard and his fate — painful enough for her to get terrible news in this way — we know more than both of them. Our historical perspective allows us to know at least in outline the whole history of Richard and what followed his deposition. We can see, as no one in the play can, not only the pathos as well as the justice of the King's imminent deposition: we can also see the consequences of that fall. Bolingbroke's unhappy reign cannot be forgotten. And Bolingbroke's original disaffection too was one of the plants Richard's misrule allowed to grow.

When the Queen steps forward, it is clear she has been

deeply pained by what she has heard: 'O, I am pressed to death through want of speaking!' (line 72). She makes quite open the point that has lain dormant since the Gardener entered; he is 'old Adam's likeness' in a garden that has been entrusted to him, but is now speculating — as Adam did, as his workman tried to — on things above his station. In her pain she sees this as paralleling Adam's Fall (lines 75ff), and this links naturally with ideas of his betrayal by the one he most trusted, Eve, and her corruption by the flattering serpent. The imaginative force of this is profound: it links to Richard a new idea that we shall see develop in the rest of the play — an idea of innocence betrayed, that he is a man more sinned against than sinning; it supports the bold subliminal linking between the (supposed) betrayal of Richard with Judas's betrayal of Christ (III.2.130–134), and pushes our idea of Richard along the road to true tragic sympathy. But the crucial thing is that the Queen sets up in our minds the Fall of Richard as the primal, Original, sin of the *Henry* plays — nothing can ever be the same again. The world is different from this point on, and only in incessant care will a shaken and wan Bolingbroke keep his hollow crown.

The Gardener's only defence is simple: what he has said is true. But again Shakespeare gives this character a way of saying it that is deliberately memorable because it has so exact and rich a visual referent. The Gardener is made to develop his news to the Queen into an elaborate conceit of scales, weights, balances, the evaluation of Bolingbroke's and Richard's 'fortunes' (line 84). Scales, of course, are as much emblematic of justice now as they were then: Richard's fall is just and necessary. But the image is also linked by line 84 with the idea of fortune, the old idea that all human life was inevitably subject to the turning of the Wheel of Fortune. This has more ambiguity than it seems at first sight. For if Richard falls as Bolingbroke rises, it not only tells us something about the conditions of Richard's life, but also reminds us that Bolingbroke is subject to fortune too. The two men are as intimately, symbiotically, related here as they are in the scales of justice, as the ivy is to the tree. Finally, this image of the reciprocal movement of the scales is an important anticipation of the image Richard himself uses of the buckets in the well as he and Bolingbroke, on opposite sides, hold the wheel-like rim of the crown. (IV.1.181ff). We recognise the similarity between the two conceits, both turning on the idea of balance and antithesis, and the earlier qualifies the later most subtly.

Plays, however attractive it is sometimes so to read them, are not academic theses or intellectual puzzles. They are also illusion — an illusion of real people, with whom our feelings are engaged. We watch the increasing pain of the Queen, a pain which causes her to curse the Gardener's labours (lines 100–101), and as we do so, something of her pain is transferred to us. Richard begins to seem much more a man to be pitied and loved than he did before, his fall to be (paradoxically) shocking and terrible as well as deserved. The agony of a loving wife and the imagery, the conceit of the whole scene, have done a great deal to modify how we look at Richard and how we understand his fate and the subsequent history of his nation. Our feelings about him are different from this moment on.

There is a final irony in the scene, which the Queen's departure easily obscures. The passion that leads her to curse is credible enough, and the Gardener takes it not in anger but in pity. His sympathy is a cue for ours — if we needed it. But he is a good gardener, who does weed out unwanted rubbish, explicitly like the Bolingbroke who 'plucked up root and all' the weeds of Bushy, Green and Wiltshire (line 52). The Gardener, symbol of the unceasing round of work from year to year, continues, one presumes, as a gardener after the change of king; and though he does not think the Queen's curse will have effect (line 103), the England in which he cultivates his garden brings forth only a bitter harvest. Bolingbroke's grafts do not take, for the Northumberland and Worcester he trusted prove false. His garden is sterile of joy and peace: his is a reign of civil war and trouble, where trenching war rather than the plough channels the fields of England and the ripening corn is flattened by the storm Richard's suffering lets loose (cf. III.3 162ff). The Queen's curse is, indeed, fulfilled. Only at the end of *Henry V*, in the great speech of Burgundy concluding peace between France and an England now at peace with itself is there any hint that the disorder in the Garden, the devastation caused by Richard's fall and murder, may be cured.

The scene, then, works on several levels. It modifies deeply how we look at Richard, but it also relates our feelings towards him to ideas of the proper management of a realm — a present question as well as one of importance when the play was new. It is therefore a parable of rule for us. For the Queen, the Gardener's speech not only discloses news to her but does it in such a way that it acts as a model, allowing her to conceptualise its importance. For the Gardener and his mate, their discourse is a deliberate and conscious analogy, not only descriptive but predictive: as in gardens, so in states.

AFTERTHOUGHT

What do you understand by 'the contemporary relevance of Shakespeare's use of English history as myth' (pages 95–96)?

2

How important is a knowledge of biblical gardens to an understanding of *Richard II*?

3

What do you understand by the idea of 'the monarch's "Two Bodies"' (page 99)?

4

'Richard's fall is just and necessary' (page 100). Do you agree?

Raman Selden

*Raman Selden is Professor of English
Literature at the University of Lancaster,
and author of numerous critical studies.*

ESSAY

Richard II and the politics of kingship

In an influential essay Nicholas Brooke argued that critics have overstated the political themes of *Richard II*, and have understated the *tragic* nature of Richard II's deposition and death. He sees Richard as 'a man caught in an impossible predicament, whose sufferings are only marginally related to his faults' (*Shakespeare's Early Tragedies*, London, 1968, pp. 122–123). I shall be arguing that the time is ripe for a newly conceived political interpretation — one which does not require us to believe that Shakespeare consciously intended to construct a political allegory. I shall not dwell on Richard's identity crisis, or upon his poetic imagination, but on the negotiations of power in which he was implicated. I shall examine the ways in which the play redefines the nature of royal power, and how it uses late medieval 'history' to rethink Elizabethan thoughts about monarchic succession and deposition. Richard's personal tragedy should not cause us to overlook the larger context of Elizabethan dynastic politics which to a great extent shaped the play's reception in its own time.

Shakespeare's *Richard II* was written in 1595 for the Chamberlain's Men as the first in a planned sequence of plays on the Lancastrian phase of dynastic history. The play proved so popular that it was published in 1597 and reprinted twice in 1598. The central theme of 'the deposing of a rightful king', to use Richard's words in the play (V.1.50), called forth numerous applications to the Elizabethan state. Fiction and reality became crucially interwoven in 1601 when, on the eve of the Essex rebellion, the followers of the Earl commissioned a performance of a play (almost certainly Shakespeare's) about Richard II's death. After the abortive coup Shakespeare's company was summoned to the trial, where it was said that Essex had enjoyed seeing the play several times.

The parallels between the play and the contemporary situation are clear enough. Elizabeth, like Richard II, was often said to have been led astray by evil counsellors, and Essex was, like Bolingbroke, a rebel and popular lord of royal blood (he was a descendant of that Duke of Gloucester whose murder was incited by Richard). She was blamed for allowing the execution of Mary Stuart, and she was attacked for 'farming' the kingdom by granting monopolies to her favourites (especially Essex and Leicester). It is recorded that, after the trial of Essex, Elizabeth told William Lambarde 'I am Richard II, know ye not that?' (*Richard II, Critical Essays*, ed. J T Newlin, New York and London, 1984, p. 3). The play treats the delicate subject of the deposition of a monarch. The sensitivity of the government can be seen in the fact that the deposition scene (IV.1) was omitted in all editions of the play printed in Elizabeth's lifetime, although it is probable that it was always included on stage (see Andrew Gurr's edition, Cambridge, 1984, p. 10).

These facts open up a perspective on the play which is in harmony with a number of modern approaches to literary criticism. First, it is clear that interpretations of the play depend to a great extent on the context in which it is staged or read. There is no ascertainable authorised meaning which is fixed for all time at the point of composition and which is determined solely by the author's intention. Attempts have been made by E D Hirsch (in *Validity in Interpretation*, New Haven and London, 1967) and others to give a special and distinct authority to the author's intention as opposed to subsequent interpretations, but they have failed to hold water. This is not to say that the play can mean just anything, but rather that its meaning will depend on the total cultural, social and economic context in which interpretation takes place. It would be easy to say that the meaning given to the play during the time of the Essex rebellion was a distorted and subjective one. However, it can also be argued that by reading a play in specific historical contexts we can bring out meanings in it which would otherwise remain only latent. Let us be clear. Shakespeare may well not have intended an allusion to Essex in his handling of Bolingbroke, but the possibility of such an application was inevitable given the current discussion, concerning deposition, the frequent parallels drawn between Elizabeth and Richard II, and the worries about the succession. Indeed, Bolingbroke's popularity, in Richard's bitter account (I.4.20ff), resembles Essex's in the early 1590s. The play must be seen as part of a substantial body of discourses upon the political history of England. Lily Campbell put her finger on the issue when she weighed the significance of the fact that the Chamberlain's Men were summoned to the trial of Essex to discuss possible contemporary applications of Richard II's story. She concludes that this shows 'the Elizabethan recognition of history as a political mirror potentially dangerous.' (Lily B Campbell, *Shakespeare's 'Histories': Mirrors of Elizabethan Policy*, London, 1964, p. 189)

Some earlier historians of literature have treated Shakespeare's plays as embodiments of orthodox Tudor and Stuart values. Following their lead, producers of the play have sometimes stressed the conservative message of the entire tetralogy. According to this older view, Richard, despite his hopelessly unkingly behaviour, is a tragic hero, whose deposition by Bolingbroke cannot be justified. The 'Homilie against Disobedience and Wilful Rebellion' (printed in Gurr's edition, pp. 215–220) was included in the book of homilies which was read in every church in the land on every Sunday and holy day during Elizabeth's reign. Several passages in it are relevant to the play. First the divine right of rulers is asserted: 'it is most evident that Kings, Queenes, and other Princes . . . are ordeined of GOD, are to be obeyed and honoured of their subects'. In the play Richard declares: 'Not all the water in the rough rude sea/ Can wash the balm off from an anointed king' (III.2.54–55). Secondly, particular attention is given to the problem of bad rulers, since it is obvious that people most often rebel against them. Bad rulers are declared to be the result of bad subjects:

'the further and further that an earthly prince doth swerve from the example of the heavenly government, the greater plague is he of GODS wrath, and punishment by GODS justice, unto that countrey and people, over whom GOD for their sinnes hath placed such a Prince and governour.' Finally, only one proper response to bad rulers is allowed: 'let us patiently suffer and obey such as wee deserve'. There can be no justification for rebellion.

The Bishop of Carlisle prophesies that Bolingbroke's usurpation of the crown will bring about 'disorder, horror, fear, and mutiny' (IV.1.142). The ensuing plays in the tetralogy continue to confirm his predictions, until Bolingbroke's son (Henry V) brings an end to disorder in the final play by successfully diverting English energies into war against the French. Bolingbroke's father, John of Gaunt, is the first to take up the orthodox beliefs of the Homilie when he refuses to take revenge on Richard for causing Gloucester's death:

> God's is the quarrel; for God's substitute,
> His deputy anointed in His sight,
> Hath caused his death; the which if wrongfully,
> Let heaven revenge, for I may never lift
> An angry arm against His minister.

> (I.2.37–41)

Carlisle expresses the traditional position simply: 'What subject can give sentence on his king?' (IV.1.121).

However, the Divine Right views are clearly not left unchallenged in the play. No one tries to refute the doctrine, but the realities of power combined with the appeal to the rights of the subject override the force of theological argument. The wrongdoings of the King — his involvement in Gloucester's death, his favouritism, and his 'farming' of the kingdom — are often recited. Forty years after the Essex rebellion, Parliament led the 'Great Rebellion' which utterly rejected the advice and perspective of the Homilie. The outcome was the execution of Charles I in 1649. It is therefore hardly surprising that many modern literary critics have seen the seeds of these rebellious attitudes in the plays of Shakespeare. Critics, such as Stephen Greenblatt, Jonathan Goldberg, Jonathan Dollimore, John Drakakis, Alan Sinfield, and Catherine Belsey, have suggested that Elizabethan and Jacobean drama is more complex and open in its political discourses than was previously thought, and that the plays include subversive voices which are not always contradicted or negated by the more orthodox opinions expressed in the plays. No one claims that Shakespeare was a radical; censorship would have silenced a truly revolutionary drama. However, the dramatic form is especially marked by openness or 'indeterminacy': orthodox values are brought into collision with subversive attitudes in ways which do not allow the construction of unequivocal solutions. Dramatic dialogue lacks even the degree of authorial comment which is possible in fiction or poetry.

Many of the play's uncertainties are centred upon York, who is the play's most compromised figure: he attacks Richard for the wrongs done to Bolingbroke, but he is still appointed Richard's deputy during the Irish campaign, before finally and reluctantly joining Bolingbroke. He points out the folly of Richard's behaviour:

> Take Hereford's rights away, and take from Time
> His charters and his customary rights.
> Let not tomorrow then ensue today.
> Be not thyself; for how art thou a king
> But by fair sequence and succession?

> (II.1.195–199)

At first York's argument seems perfectly traditional: Bolingbroke's hereditary rights, crudely seized by Richard, are part of the divinely ordained social system of feudal England. Interfere with this order at any point and the whole thing will collapse. York points out that Richard's own position is buttressed by the same timeless sanctions. By trampling upon feudal rights, Richard is undermining his own position: 'Be not thyself'. However, this logic also destroys the fundamental tenet of the Homilie, which asserts that only God can correct a foolish king, and that subjects can only pray (compare Gaunt's 'God's is the quarrel', I.2.37). In acting as he does, Richard is *deposing himself*. This goes against Carlisle's argument that the king cannot resign his office (IV.1.121ff). However, even Gaunt, despite his unquestioning loyalty, opens up, in the word-play of his deathbed scene, a view of Richard which undercuts his authority. Gaunt tells Richard: 'thou . . . art possessed now to depose thyself' (II.1.107–108). 'Depose' means 'disinherit', but also introduces the inevitable political sense. Gaunt goes on to comment on Richard's destruction of his own legal position: 'Landlord of England art thou now, not king./ Thy state of law is bondslave to the law' (II.1.113–114). A king should be above the law, but Richard has placed himself beneath it. Finally, a king should be above moral comparisons. York, entrusted with the kingdom, despairs of coping, because his allegiance is divided:

> Both are my kinsmen.
> T'one is my sovereign, whom both my oath
> And duty bids defend. T'other again
> Is my kinsman, whom the King hath wronged,
> Whom conscience and my kindred bids to right.
>
> (II.2.111–115)

This even-handed weighing of moral obligations is itself a significant departure from the unequivocal demands of loyalty required by the Homilie. Behind York's uncertain and wavering attitudes a new and highly disturbing principle is emerging: *a king may render himself unworthy of office*. Even when he tries to reassert the Divine Right attitude, reminding Bolingbroke that 'the heavens are over our heads', the latter smoothly deflects the criticism: 'I know it, uncle, and oppose not myself/ Against their will' (III.3.17–19). This new Hobbesian monarch, whose justice derives from superior power, claims to be observing God's will in putting the realm to rights. As Northumberland comments, Bolingbroke will 'make high majesty look like itself' (II.1.295). The medieval doctrine of the king's 'Two Bodies' (the separation of the king's physical body from his spiritual or legal one) does much to sustain Richard's tragic status in the play, but it also tends to undermine his authority. The doctrine was used to excuse the weaknesses of individual monarchs (however unworthy they are as private persons, their kingship remains untarnished), but could equally be used to point up the theoretical *separability* of person and office. In *Richard II* we see a traditional logic undoing (deconstructing) itself before our eyes.

A rather different perspective on the play is afforded by the work of Stephen Greenblatt, who argues that Shakespeare's history plays develop and explore the structures of Tudor monarchic politics. He shows that royal power maintains itself not simply by imposing its authority but by permitting a controlled subversion of that authority. That is, the ruler permits the expression of subversive views only in order to contain the subversion. To some extent this is a safety-valve view of power: you allow carnivals and anti-government demonstrations because they exhaust the power of subversion. However, Greenblatt takes his argument further when he declares: 'Indeed subversiveness is the very product of that power and furthers its ends' (*Shakespearean Negotiations*, Berkeley and Los Angeles, 1988, p. 30). On this view, demonstrations are encouraged because they have the effect of legitimating the authority which uses its power to contain them. He applies this very intelligently to the next play in the tetralogy, *Henry IV, Part 1*, in which Hal, Bolingbroke's son, places himself in the world of the potentially subversive tavern-dwellers only to assert his authority over behaviour which he had appeared to condone.

However, Richard II is a king who subverts his own authority from the beginning out of sheer incompetence. We can sustain Greenblatt's perspective only if we see the play as enacting a larger scheme of monarchic self-justification, and not just the destiny of a single tragic figure. Bolingbroke possesses the kingly qualities which Richard lacks. For example, he has that familiar relationship with the common people which Hal exploits in *Henry IV, Part 1*. Richard observes his 'courtship to the common people,/ How he did seem to dive into their hearts' (I.4.24–25). The decisiveness of his authority when he stands in royal judgement of Bagot and Aumerle (IV.1) contrasts with Richard's vacillations in the first scene ('We were not born to sue, but to command;/ Which, since we cannot do. . .' I.1.196–197). Richard cedes the crown to Bolingbroke without being asked. In the scene at Flint Castle, Bolingbroke formally confirms his allegiance and requests only the restoration of his lands and title, but Richard simply capitulates: 'What must the King do now? Must he submit?/ The King shall do it. Must he be deposed?/ The King shall be contented.' (III.3.143–145). For all Richard's eloquent assertions of his divine authority, the power of monarchy passes from him almost voluntarily. He never acknowledges Bolingbroke's right to take it, and Boling-broke never demands it until it is offered. However, underlying the formal discourse is the discourse of power. Richard has undermined his own authority from the beginning and has thereby justified its usurpation by Bolingbroke. In general terms, monarchical power has undermined itself only to justify itself. Henry IV is the king Richard II should have been. The dreadful disorder which is threatened by the very idea of deposition is contained and managed in the play's compact chan-nelling of power from unwise ruler to kingly usurper. Despite the disorders which follow, the overall movement of the tetralogy is towards the established monarchical authority of Henry V. In the process, the idea of the divine right of kings undergoes some weakening, and this is undoubtedly important when we consider what was to happen fifty years later. But, for the moment, royal power has been re-legitimated. As Terence Hawkes has put it, 'The king is rejected, but not kingship' (*Shakespeare's Talking Animals*, London, 1973, p. 75). It is clear that this accommodation within the system of monarchical government opened up a dangerous gap in its defences.

I have been arguing that the play is a relatively open text which allows different constructions to be placed upon it. This applies especially to the political meanings which were derived from it during the period of Shakespeare's life. Secondly, I have suggested that, despite the weakening of the older divine right view of monarchy in the play, the king's authority is preserved by an appeal to power and efficiency. Richard's weaknesses serve only to justify Henry's usurpation and to promote the new Hobbesian image of the monarch. Finally, we cannot ignore the long-term effects of this subtle adjustment in the ways in which monarchy effected its self-legitimation. After all, Charles I was another foolish king, who believed he could sustain his divine right to rule, but his claims were rudely denied at the scaffold in 1649.

AFTERTHOUGHTS

1

Does a 'political interpretation' (page 104) of *Richard II* necessarily deny Richard tragic status?

2

Do you agree that in *Richard II*, 'The king is rejected, but not kingship' (page 111)?

3

What significance does Selden attach to the fact that *Richard II* was played immediately before the Essex rebellion?

4

Compare the discussion of kingship in this essay with Draper's comments on pages 80–84.

Cedric Watts

Cedric Watts is Professor of English at Sussex University, and author of many scholarly publications.

ESSAY

Transtextual aspects of *Richard II*

No, I don't like the word 'transtextual' either, but it's very useful for the purposes of this essay. A transtextual story is one which extends across two or more texts. The word 'contextual' won't do, because it leads too rapidly away from *Richard II*. 'Transtextual', on the other hand, suggests not only ways in which *Richard II* leads to other works but also ways in which other works have a reciprocally transforming effect on *Richard II*. If you read that drama on its own, you'll misjudge it; if you regard it as a drama which is part of a sequence, it becomes better: more pointed, more complex, more ironic.

When Shakespeare wrote what its earliest printed text terms *The Tragedie of King Richard the Second*, he envisaged the possibility that it would be followed by at least two sequels, one dealing with the troubled reign of Henry IV, another dealing with the successful reign of Henry V. He probably foresaw the main outlines of those subsequent works but had not foreseen their detail. In the event, his story of the troubled reign of Henry IV proved to contain so much fruitful material that there emerged two full-length plays, *Henry IV, Part 1* and *Henry IV, Part 2* before that dealing with Henry V's successes.

Within the text of *Richard II* there is clear evidence that

E

Shakespeare foresaw likely sequels. For instance, some details of the play may at first seem to be unnecessary 'loose ends' or needless elaborations. But they prove to be important thematic and narrative preludes to the material of future plays. One of these apparently unnecessary features is that Harry Percy (alias 'Hotspur'), Northumberland's son, appears in Act II, scene 3, and is introduced at some length to Bolingbroke, whom he promises to serve loyally. Given that Hotspur has no important role in the plot of *Richard II* but is merely one of numerous supporters of Bolingbroke, the detailed introduction may seem superfluous. One reason for the careful presentation of Hotspur is that he will figure prominently in the next play, *1 Henry IV*; and when we see that in that play he is the most valiant of the rebels against the new king (Bolingbroke being now Henry IV), we see that a retrospective ironic light is shed on that scene in *Richard II* in which he had promised his true and constant allegiance to the usurper. Another telling detail is that as soon as Bolingbroke comes to power, we hear the new ruler express domestic worries: in particular, his fear that his son is proving dissolute and disloyal:

> Can no man tell me of my unthrifty son?
> 'Tis full three months since I did see him last.
> If any plague hang over us, 'tis he.
> I would to God, my lords, he might be found.
> Inquire at London 'mongst the taverns there;
> For there, they say, he daily doth frequent
> With unrestrainèd loose companions

(V.3.1–7)

Bolingbroke's son does not appear in person in *Richard II*; but this speech by Bolingbroke serves as a prelude to *1 Henry IV*, in which we will be shown extensively the life that that son, Hal, is leading in the taverns among such 'unrestrainèd loose companions' as Falstaff and Poins. Bolingbroke remarks in *Richard II* that he perceives in Hal 'some sparks of better hope, which elder years/ May happily bring forth'; and these words portend the gradual emergence, in *1* and *2 Henry IV*, of Hal as a truly valiant and noble heir to the throne. The combination of the detailed introduction of Hotspur and the expression of paternal fears about Hal's character shows that before *Richard*

II was completed, Shakespeare was already thinking ahead to a work in which much of the interest was to depend on the character-contrast between two Harries: Harry Percy (Hotspur) and Harry Monmouth (Hal). As a matter of historical fact, Hotspur was more than twenty years older than Hal; Shakespeare chooses to suggest that they are much the same age as each other, so as to invite us to see them in *1 Henry IV* as comparable and contrasting young rivals for power. This process of comparison is inaugurated in *Richard II* when we see Hotspur as the apparently loyal henchman of Bolingbroke and hear that Hal is the apparently wayward son. Later events, in which Hal proves loyal and Hotspur rebellious, cast a retrospective irony upon these details of *Richard II*.

In the main action of *Richard II*, we are shown how Richard is deposed by Henry Bolingbroke, and Bolingbroke becomes King Henry IV; but we also hear grim prophecies that the downfall of Richard, 'the Lord's anointed' (a rightful king who is therefore God's deputy on earth), will inevitably bring divine wrath upon the head of the usurper. Both the Bishop of Carlisle and Richard himself offer predictions that if Bolingbroke gains the throne, his reign will be an era of appalling and extensive civil war. When we hear such predictions, we naturally wonder whether the speakers do indeed have prophetic insight into the future; and in the subsequent plays we see that the predictions were prophecies which are amply fulfilled. Furthermore their fulfilment is very systematically emphasised by Shakespeare. For instance, in *Richard II*, Richard tells the Earl of Northumberland:

> Northumberland, thou ladder wherewithal
> The mounting Bolingbroke ascends my throne,
> The time shall not be many hours of age
> More than it is ere foul sin, gathering head,
> Shall break into corruption. Thou shalt think,
> Though he divide the realm and give thee half,
> It is too little, helping him to all.

(V.1.55–61)

In *1 Henry IV*, the prophecy is fulfilled: we see that Northumberland, who had helped Bolingbroke to power, is now conspiring against him; and in *2 Henry IV*, the conspiracy continues, and Henry actually quotes (very closely if not exactly) Richard's words:

> But which of you was by —
> (*To Warwick*) You, cousin Nevil, as I may remember —
> When Richard, with his eye brimful of tears,
> Then checked and rated by Northumberland,
> Did speak these words, now proved a prophecy?
> 'Northumberland, thou ladder by the which
> My cousin Bolingbroke ascends my throne' —
> Though then, God knows, I had no such intent
> But that necessity so bowed the state
> That I and greatness were compelled to kiss —
> 'The time shall come' — thus did he follow it —
> 'The time will come that foul sin, gathering head,
> Shall break into corruption' — so went on,
> Foretelling this same time's condition,
> And the division of our amity.
>
> (III.1.65–79)

So the plays *1* and *2 Henry IV*, emphasise that the dire prophecies by the Bishop of Carlisle and particularly by Richard have indeed been fulfilled. And clearly this affects, retrospectively, our judgement of King Richard himself. In the first half of the play *Richard II*, we may rightly feel highly critical of him: he's an irresponsible, egoistic figure, capable of cynicism and callousness (as in his responsibility for Woodstock's death and his contempt for the dying Gaunt). In his downfall, he displays qualities of introspective sensitivity which, though often tainted by self-pitying dramatisation, may help to win our sympathy for him. At the time of his murder, he fights valiantly though outnumbered, and dies courageously. So he gradually rises in our estimation. But what is particularly remarkable is that his stature continues to increase after his death. In the subsequent plays, we see that his prophecies of terrible civil war are amply fulfilled. This invests him with prophetic stature, and increases the sense that though Richard was certainly fallible and sinful as a man, he still had sanctity conferred on him by his office as the rightful and consecrated King of England. Shakespeare underlines this point by letting later characters recall explicitly those early prophecies. In this way, Shakespeare is supporting the official Elizabethan political view that rebellion against a rightful king is a sacrilegious act — a defiance of God. For Elizabethans, politics had a religious dimension; indeed, religion and politics constituted one large turbulent discourse of power.

The feeling that the deposition and killing of Richard II was a sacrilegious act is emphasised at the end of *Richard II* and is greatly reinforced in the subsequent three plays. On hearing of the death of Richard, Bolingbroke (now Henry IV) says:

> I'll make a voyage to the Holy Land,
> To wash this blood off from my guilty hand.
>
> (V.6.49–50)

In *1* and *2 Henry IV*, we see that he never succeeds in making this penitential pilgrimage, and that's because he is constantly beset by rebellions at home. Nevertheless, there is a sense in which he does succeed in reaching Jerusalem. In *2 Henry IV* he suffers a fatal stroke; when dying, he enquires the name of the chamber in which he was afflicted. The chamber, he is told, is 'called Jerusalem'. He responds:

> Laud be to God! even there my life must end.
> It hath been prophesied to me, many years,
> I should not die but in Jerusalem,
> Which vainly I supposed the Holy Land.
> But bear me to that chamber; there I'll lie;
> In that Jerusalem shall Harry die.
>
> (IV.5.234–239)

So the reference to 'the Holy Land' in *Richard II* gains, with hindsight, a powerfully ironic resonance when we know the precise circumstances of the death of Henry IV.

Although a stroke may be the immediate cause of Henry's death, *2 Henry IV* gives the impression that he is driven to death mainly by sheer weariness induced by the cares of state, and in particular his worries as he contends with rebellion after rebellion. As the rebels themselves point out, it was he who set their example: by usurping the throne of a king he has created a precedent for others. He spends sleepless nights, envying the slumbers enjoyed by humble subjects (III.1.4–31). In *Henry V* we see that his son, too, is a sleepless, worried monarch, who envies the slumbers of the humble (IV.1.272–290). In both plays the wakefulness induced by cares of state is linked to guilt at the deposition of Richard. Henry V may seem to be a splendidly successful monarch, uniting the different parts of the realm beneath his banner when he goes abroad to fight the French; but on the eve of the Battle of Agincourt, after walking amongst the troops, he reflects bitterly on the guilt he has inherited with the ill-gotten throne:

> Not today, O Lord,
> O not today, think not upon the fault
> My father made in compassing the crown!
> I Richard's body have interrèd new,
> And on it have bestowed more contrite tears
> Than from it issued forcèd drops of blood.
> Five hundred poor I have in yearly pay,
> Who twice a year their withered hands hold up
> Toward heaven, to pardon blood: and I have built
> Two chantries where the sad and solemn priests
> Sing still for Richard's soul. More will I do,
> Though all that I can do is nothing worth,
> Since that my penitence comes after all,
> Imploring pardon.

(IV.1.285–298)

In the event, it appears that God has, at last, decided to pardon the Lancasters for their usurpation. At the Battle of Agincourt, the English gain an apparently miraculous victory over the far more numerous French forces. 'O God, thy arm was here', says the grateful King Henry. But a long and bloody era has elapsed before, eventually, Henry V can rest secure. Richard had cast a long and ominous shadow over the usurpers. The effect of these subsequent plays, then, is greatly to magnify, and endorse, Richard's sense that though as man he was culpable, as lawful king he was God's deputy on earth. It could be said that Shakespeare's story of Richard is not completed until Act V of *Henry V*. In thematic, political and religious terms, the four dramas from *Richard II* to *Henry V* constitute a subtly coherent and richly ironic tetralogy.

There's another important way in which the later plays transform our understanding of *Richard II*. That drama is conspicuously poetical. It contains no prose; much of the verse

is blank verse, but a substantial proportion of the verse is in
rhyming couplets. Furthermore, the poetry is frequently of a
rather formal or ceremonial kind. It has sufficient dramatic
liveliness, and the main characters are portrayed with ample
strength. Nevertheless, there are numerous occasions which
seem highly stylised, so that utterances seem formalised rather
than realistically spontaneous. Gaunt on his deathbed retains
sufficient energy to offer a remarkably choric patriotic speech
on England as:

> This royal throne of kings, this sceptred isle,
> This earth of majesty, this seat of Mars,
> This other Eden — demi-paradise

(II.1.40–42)

As for the Gardener in Act III, scene 4, he speaks like no real
gardener but like another choric commentator. With stately
eloquence he offers an elaborate analogy between good
gardening and good statecraft, explaining that Richard had
failed to prune, weed and lop in the 'garden' which is the realm
of England. (He even knows more about current affairs of state,
including Richard's downfall, than does the Queen herself.) So
in various ways the styles employed in *Richard II* emphasise the
formal and ceremonial. *1* and *2 Henry IV* offer some strong
contrasts. These plays contain a great deal of prose, and the
verse tends on the whole to be more dramatic and less conspicuously formal. Now you could explain this contrast by saying
that in the course of his development as a dramatist, Shakespeare's writing tended to become more flexibly expressive, more
psychologically vivid; he moved away from relatively formal to
relatively realistic utterance. This broad pattern of development
does not fully account, however, for the marked shift between
Richard II and the subsequent two plays, given that their likely
dates are (respectively) 1595, 1597 and 1597: in the space of two
years, the 'maturing' of the styles seems very rapid. E M W
Tillyard[1] has explained the difference by suggesting that Shakespeare wished to emphasise, in the very modes of discourse, a
contrast between the 'medieval' world of *Richard II* and the new

---

[1] *Shakespeare's History Plays* (Harmondsworth, 1962), pp. 244–261.

'modern' world which was inaugurated by Henry IV. Shakespeare often associates legitimate order with ceremonial utterance; so *Richard II* will contain much of it. With the deposition of the rightful king, we enter a new era of 'pragmatic' rather than 'sacred' monarchy; and, in any case, that new era will for a long time be turbulent and riven with conflict. The more flexible and relatively realistic modes of *1* and *2 Henry IV* express at the stylistic level a change in world-view, a 'fall' into a credibly familiar political world. Although I am not fully convinced by Tillyard's theory (which does not work for *every* scene), I think that there is *some* truth in it, for in Shakespeare's plays we can often see some co-ordination between (on the one hand) an orderly state and orderly utterance and (on the other hand) a disorderly state and disorderly utterance. It follows that much of the conspicuously ornate and formal rhetoric of *Richard II* may be more subtly functional than it first appears to be; political themes may be implicit in the very rhythms of the verse.

Bolingbroke may have been punished, by guilt and rebellion, for his desposition of Richard, but it could be argued that the eventual outcome was good, for the reign of Henry V is depicted by Shakespeare as remarkably successful: the realm is united, the French are defeated, and security seems assured by a dynastic marriage between Henry and the French princess, Katharine. At the end of *Henry V*, however, the Chorus sounds a warning. It tells us that Henry's reign was short and that the era of his successor, Henry VI, was a wretched era of civil war — 'Which oft our stage hath shown'. Thus, the Chorus reminds the audience that the later reign, that of Henry VI, has already been enacted in the theatre in the *Henry VI* trilogy by William Shakespeare; a trilogy whose sequel was the play *Richard III*. So it is not only the case that *Richard II* can be regarded as the first play in a tetralogy; it's also the case that the Chorus invites us to link that tetralogy to *another*, which, though it concerns subsequent events, had actually been performed previously. The imaginative effect is to turn a historical sequence into a cycle. In Act V of *Henry V* we may feel that after so much turmoil, British history has at last reached a glorious time of peace and prosperity. The final chorus undermines that sense of progressive evolution from the age of Richard II, and introduces a daunting sense that history is cyclical: after civil war, civil peace, but then civil war again; after usurpation, orderly succession, but then further usurpation.

The Earl of Essex, supported by Shakespeare's patron, the Earl of Southampton, rebelled against Queen Elizabeth in February 1601. The rebellion was unsuccessful: Essex was executed, and Southampton was jailed. It is well known that on the eve of the rebellion, Essex's supporters paid Shakespeare's company for a special performance of *Richard II*. The earliest printed texts of the play lack the deposition scene, which was apparently censored. Elizabeth is reported to have remarked angrily, 'I am Richard II, know ye not that?'. Shakespeare's play may have dealt with events of the fourteenth century; but it was also contemporaneous in reference, dealing with the real fears and ambitions of his day. If Essex's supporters had known more about 'transtextuality', they might have given more attention to the plays which followed *Richard II*, and they might then have been deterred from risking (and, in some cases, losing) their lives.

AFTERTHOUGHTS

1

Can you think of an alternative term for 'transtextual' that might clarify Watts's case?

2

'For Elizabethans, politics had a religious dimension' (page 117). Explain the importance of this statement to Watts's argument.

3

What difference does Watts identify between the style of *Richard II* and of the two *Henry IV* plays? What explanations does he offer to account for this?

4

How important is a knowledge of Shakespeare's other history plays to an understanding of *Richard II*?

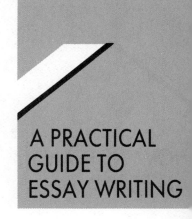

A PRACTICAL GUIDE TO ESSAY WRITING

INTRODUCTION

First, a word of warning. Good essays are the product of a creative engagement with literature. So never try to restrict your studies to what you think will be 'useful in the exam'. Ironically, you will restrict your grade potential if you do.

This doesn't mean, of course, that you should ignore the basic skills of essay writing. When you read critics, make a conscious effort to notice *how* they communicate their ideas. The guidelines that follow offer advice of a more explicit kind. But they are no substitute for practical experience. It is never easy to express ideas with clarity and precision. But the more often you tackle the problems involved and experiment to find your own voice, the more fluent you will become. So practise writing essays as often as possible.

HOW TO PLAN
AN ESSAY

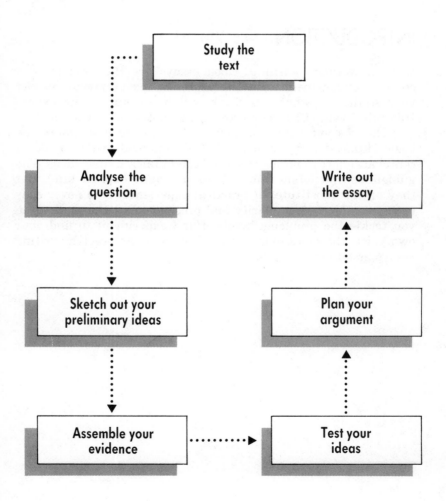

Study the
text

Analyse the
question

Write out
the essay

Sketch out your
preliminary ideas

Plan your
argument

Assemble your
evidence

Test your
ideas

Study the text

The first step in writing a good essay is to get to know the set text well. Never write about a text until you are fully familiar with it. Even a discussion of the opening chapter of a novel, for example, should be informed by an understanding of the book as a whole. Literary texts, however, are by their very nature complex and on a first reading you are bound to miss many significant features. Re-read the book with care, if possible more than once. Look up any unfamiliar words in a good dictionary and if the text you are studying was written more than a few decades ago, consult the *Oxford English Dictionary* to find out whether the meanings of any terms have shifted in the intervening period.

Good books are difficult to put down when you first read them. But a more leisurely second or third reading gives you the opportunity to make notes on those features you find significant. An index of characters and events is often useful, particularly when studying novels with a complex plot or time scheme. The main aim, however, should be to record your *responses* to the text. By all means note, for example, striking images. But be sure to add *why* you think them striking. Similarly, record any thoughts you may have on interesting comparisons with other texts, puzzling points of characterisation, even what you take to be aesthetic blemishes. The important thing is to annotate fully and adventurously. The most seemingly idiosyncratic comment may later lead to a crucial area of discussion which you would otherwise have overlooked. It helps to have a working copy of the text in which to mark up key passages and jot down marginal comments (although obviously these practices are taboo when working with library, borrowed or valuable copies!). But keep a fuller set of notes as well and organise these under appropriate headings.

Literature does not exist in an aesthetic vacuum, however, and you should try to find out as much as possible about the context of its production and reception. It is particularly important to read other works by the same author and writings by contemporaries. At this early stage, you may want to restrict your secondary reading to those standard reference works, such as biographies, which are widely available in public libraries. In the long run, however, it pays to read as wide a range of critical studies as possible.

Some students, and tutors, worry that such studies may stifle the development of any truly personal response. But this won't happen if you are alert to the danger and read critically. After all, you wouldn't passively accept what a stranger told you in conversation. The fact that a critic's views are in print does not necessarily make them any more authoritative (as a glance at the review pages of the *TLS* and *London Review of Books* will reveal). So question the views you find: 'Does this critic's interpretation agree with mine and where do we part company?' 'Can it be right to try and restrict this text's meanings to those found by its author or first audience?' 'Doesn't this passage treat a theatrical text as though it were a novel?' Often it is views which you reject which prove most valuable since they challenge you to articulate your own position with greater clarity. Be sure to keep careful notes on what the critic wrote, and your *reactions* to what the critic wrote.

Analyse the question

You cannot begin to answer a question until you understand what task it is you have been asked to perform. Re-cast the question in your own words and reconstruct the line of reasoning which lies behind it. Where there is a choice of topics, try to choose the one for which you are best prepared. It would, for example, be unwise to tackle 'How far do you agree that in *Paradise Lost* Milton transformed the epic models he inherited from ancient Greece and Rome?' without a working knowledge of Homer and Virgil (or *Paradise Lost* for that matter!). If you do not already know the works of these authors, the question should spur you on to read more widely — or discourage you from attempting it at all. The scope of an essay, however, is not always so obvious and you must remain alert to the implied demands of each question. How could you possibly 'Consider the view that *Wuthering Heights* transcends the conventions of the Gothic novel' without reference to at least some of those works which, the question suggests, have *not* transcended Gothic conventions?

When you have decided on a topic, analyse the terms of the question itself. Sometimes these self-evidently require careful definition: *tragedy* and *irony*, for example, are notoriously difficult concepts to pin down and you will probably need to consult a good dictionary of literary terms. Don't ignore, however, those seemingly innocuous phrases which often smuggle in significant assumptions. 'Does Macbeth lack the nobility of the true tragic hero?' obviously invites you to discuss nobility and the nature of the tragic hero. But what of 'lack' and 'true' — do they suggest that the play would be improved had Shakespeare depicted Macbeth in a different manner? or that tragedy is superior to other forms of drama? Remember that you are not expected meekly to agree with the assumptions implicit in the question. Some questions are deliberately provocative in order to stimulate an engaged response. Don't be afraid to take up the challenge.

Sketch out your preliminary ideas

'Which comes first, the evidence or the answer?' is one of those chicken and egg questions. How can you form a view without inspecting the evidence? But how can you know which evidence is relevant without some idea of what it is you are looking for? In practice the mind reviews evidence and formulates preliminary theories or hypotheses at one and the same time, although for the sake of clarity we have separated out the processes. Remember that these early ideas are only there to get you started. You *expect* to modify them in the light of the evidence you uncover. Your initial hypothesis may be an instinctive 'gut-reaction'. Or you may find that you prefer to 'sleep on the problem', allowing ideas to gell over a period of time. Don't worry in either case. The mind is quite capable of processing a vast amount of accumulated evidence, the product of previous reading and thought, and reaching sophisticated intuitive judgements. Eventually, however, you are going to have to think carefully through any ideas you arrive at by such intuitive processes. Are they logical? Do they take account of all the relevant factors? Do they fully answer the question set? Are there any obvious reasons to qualify or abandon them?

Assemble your evidence

Now is the time to return to the text and re-read it with the question and your working hypothesis firmly in mind. Many of the notes you have already made are likely to be useful, but assess the precise relevance of this material and make notes on any new evidence you discover. The important thing is to cast your net widely and take into account points which tend to undermine your case as well as those that support it. As always, ensure that your notes are full, accurate, and reflect your own critical judgements.

You may well need to go outside the text if you are to do full justice to the question. If you think that the 'Oedipus complex' may be relevant to an answer on *Hamlet* then read Freud and a balanced selection of those critics who have discussed the appropriateness of applying psychoanalytical theories to the interpretation of literature. Their views can most easily be tracked down by consulting the annotated bibliographies held by most major libraries (and don't be afraid to ask a librarian for help in finding and using these). Remember that you go to works of criticism not only to obtain information but to stimulate you into clarifying your own position. And that since life is short and many critical studies are long, judicious use of a book's index and/or contents list is not to be scorned. You can save yourself a great deal of future labour if you carefully record full bibliographic details at this stage.

Once you have collected the evidence, organise it coherently. Sort the detailed points into related groups and identify the quotations which support these. You must also assess the relative importance of each point, for in an essay of limited length it is essential to establish a firm set of priorities, exploring some ideas in depth while discarding or subordinating others.

Test your ideas

As we stressed earlier, a hypothesis is only a proposal, and one that you fully expect to modify. Review it with the evidence before you. Do you really still believe in it? It would be surprising if you did not want to modify it in some way. If you cannot see any problems, others may. Try discussing your ideas with friends and relatives. Raise them in class discussions. Your tutor is certain to welcome your initiative. The critical process is essentially collaborative and there is absolutely no reason why you should not listen to and benefit from the views of others. Similarly, you should feel free to test your ideas against the theories put forward in academic journals and books. But do not just borrow what you find. Critically analyse the views on offer and, where appropriate, integrate them into your own pattern of thought. You must, of course, give full acknowledgement to the sources of such views.

Do not despair if you find you have to abandon or modify significantly your initial position. The fact that you are prepared to do so is a mark of intellectual integrity. Dogmatism is never an academic virtue and many of the best essays explore the *process* of scholarly enquiry rather than simply record its results.

Plan your argument

Once you have more or less decided on your attitude to the question (for an answer is never really 'finalised') you have to present your case in the most persuasive manner. In order to do this you must avoid meandering from point to point and instead produce an organised argument — a structured flow of ideas and supporting evidence, leading logically to a conclusion which fully answers the question. Never begin to write until you have produced an outline of your argument.

You may find it easiest to begin by sketching out its main stage as a flow chart or some other form of visual presentation. But eventually you should produce a list of paragraph topics. The paragraph is the conventional written demarcation for a unit of thought and you can outline an argument quite simply by briefly summarising the substance of each paragraph and then checking that these points (you may remember your English teacher referring to them as topic sentences) really do follow a coherent order. Later you will be able to elaborate on each topic, illustrating and qualifying it as you go along. But you will find this far easier to do if you possess from the outset a clear map of where you are heading.

All questions require some form of an argument. Even so-called 'descriptive' questions *imply* the need for an argument. An adequate answer to the request to 'Outline the role of Iago in *Othello*' would do far more than simply list his appearances on stage. It would at the very least attempt to provide some *explanation* for his actions — is he, for example, a representative stage 'Machiavel'? an example of pure evil, 'motiveless malignity'? or a realistic study of a tormented personality reacting to identifiable social and psychological pressures?

Your conclusion ought to address the terms of the question. It may seem obvious, but 'how far do you agree', 'evaluate', 'consider', 'discuss', etc, are *not* interchangeable formulas and your conclusion must take account of the precise wording of the question. If asked 'How far do you agree?', the concluding paragraph of your essay really should state whether you are in complete agreement, total disagreement, or, more likely, partial agreement. Each preceding paragraph should have a clear justification for its existence and help to clarify the reasoning which underlies your conclusion. If you find that a paragraph serves no good purpose (perhaps merely summarising the plot), do not hesitate to discard it.

The arrangement of the paragraphs, the overall strategy of the argument, can vary. One possible pattern is dialectical: present the arguments in favour of one point of view (**thesis**); then turn to counter-arguments or to a rival interpretation (**antithesis**); finally evaluate the competing claims and arrive at your own conclusion (**synthesis**). You may, on the other hand, feel so convinced of the merits of one particular case that you wish to devote your entire essay to arguing that viewpoint persuasively (although it is always desirable to indicate, however briefly, that you are aware of alternative, if flawed, positions). As the essays contained in this volume demonstrate, there are many other possible strategies. Try to adopt the one which will most comfortably accommodate the demands of the question and allow you to express your thoughts with the greatest possible clarity.

Be careful, however, not to apply abstract formulas in a mechanical manner. It is true that you should be careful to define your terms. It is *not* true that every essay should begin with 'The dictionary defines *x* as . . .'. In fact, definitions are often best left until an appropriate moment for their introduction arrives. Similarly every essay should have a beginning, middle and end. But it does not follow that in your opening paragraph you should announce an intention to write an essay, or that in your concluding paragraph you need to signal an imminent desire to put down your pen. The old adages are often useful reminders of what constitutes good practice, but they must be interpreted intelligently.

Write out the essay

Once you have developed a coherent argument you should aim to communicate it in the most effective manner possible. Make certain you clearly identify yourself, and the question you are answering. Ideally, type your answer, or at least ensure your handwriting is legible and that you leave sufficient space for your tutor's comments. Careless presentation merely distracts from the force of your argument. Errors of grammar, syntax and spelling are far more serious. At best they are an irritating blemish, particularly in the work of a student who should be sensitive to the nuances of language. At worst, they seriously confuse the sense of your argument. If you are aware that you have stylistic problems of this kind, ask your tutor for advice at the earliest opportunity. Everyone, however, is liable to commit the occasional howler. The only remedy is to give yourself plenty of time in which to proof-read your manuscript (often reading it aloud is helpful) before submitting it.

Language, however, is not only an instrument of communication; it is also an instrument of thought. If you want to think clearly and precisely you should strive for a clear, precise prose style. Keep your sentences short and direct. Use modern, straightforward English wherever possible. Avoid repetition, clichés and wordiness. Beware of generalisations, simplifications, and overstatements. Orwell analysed the relationship between stylistic vice and muddled thought in his essay 'Politics and the English Language' (1946) — it remains essential reading (and is still readily available in volume 4 of the Penguin *Collected Essays, Journalism and Letters*). Generalisations, for example, are always dangerous. They are rarely true and tend to suppress the individuality of the texts in question. A remark such as 'Keats always employs sensuous language in his poetry' is not only fatuous (what, after all, does it mean? is *every* word he wrote equally 'sensuous'?) but tends to obscure interesting distinctions which could otherwise be made between, say, the descriptions in the 'Ode on a Grecian Urn' and those in 'To Autumn'.

The intelligent use of quotations can help you make your points with greater clarity. Don't sprinkle them throughout your essay without good reason. There is no need, for example, to use them to support uncontentious statements of fact. 'Macbeth murdered Duncan' does not require textual evidence (unless you wish to dispute Thurber's brilliant parody, 'The Macbeth Murder Mystery', which reveals Lady Macbeth's father as the culprit!). Quotations should be included, however, when they are necessary to support your case. The proposition that Macbeth's imaginative powers wither after he has killed his king would certainly require extensive quotation: you would almost certainly want to analyse key passages from both before and after the murder (perhaps his first and last soliloquies?). The key word here is 'analyse'. Quotations cannot make your points on their own. It is up to you to demonstrate their relevance and clearly explain to your readers *why* you want them to focus on the passage you have selected.

Most of the academic conventions which govern the presentation of essays are set out briefly in the style sheet below. The question of gender, however, requires fuller discussion. More than half the population of the world is female. Yet many writers still refer to an undifferentiated *man*kind. Or write of the author and *his* public. We do not think that this convention has much to recommend it. At the very least, it runs the risk of introducing unintended sexist attitudes. And at times leads to such patent absurdities as 'Cleopatra's final speech asserts *man*'s true nobility'. With a little thought, you can normally find ways of expressing yourself which do not suggest that the typical author, critic or reader is male. Often you can simply use plural forms, which is probably a more elegant solution than relying on such awkward formulations as 's/he' or 'he and she'. You should also try to avoid distinguishing between male and female authors on the basis of forenames. Why *Jane* Austen and not *George* Byron? Refer to all authors by their last names unless there is some good reason not to. Where there may otherwise be confusion, say between T S and George Eliot, give the name in full when it first occurs and thereafter use the last name only.

Finally, keep your audience firmly in mind. Tutors and examiners are interested in understanding your conclusions and the processes by which you arrived at them. They are not interested in reading a potted version of a book they already know. **So don't pad out your work with plot summary.**

Hints for examinations

In an examination you should go through exactly the same processes as you would for the preparation of a term essay. The only difference lies in the fact that some of the stages will have had to take place before you enter the examination room. This should not bother you unduly. Examiners are bound to avoid the merely eccentric when they come to formulate papers and if you have read widely and thought deeply about the central issues raised by your set texts you can be confident you will have sufficient material to answer the majority of questions sensibly.

The fact that examinations impose strict time limits makes it *more* rather than less, important that you plan carefully. There really is no point in floundering into an answer without any idea of where you are going, particularly when there will not be time to recover from the initial error.

Before you begin to answer any question at all, study the entire paper with care. Check that you understand the rubric and know how many questions you have to answer and whether any are compulsory. It may be comforting to spot a title you feel confident of answering well, but don't rush to tackle it: read *all* the questions before deciding which *combination* will allow you to display your abilities to the fullest advantage. Once you have made your choice, analyse each question, sketch out your ideas, assemble the evidence, review your initial hypothesis, plan your argument, *before* trying to write out an answer. And make notes at each stage: not only will these help you arrive at a sensible conclusion, but examiners are impressed by evidence of careful thought.

Plan your time as well as your answers. If you have practised writing timed essays as part of your revision, you should not find this too difficult. There can be a temptation to allocate extra time to the questions you know you can answer well; but this is always a short-sighted policy. You will find yourself left to face a question which would in any event have given you difficulty without even the time to give it serious thought. It is, moreover, easier to gain marks at the lower end of the scale than at the upper, and you will never compensate for one poor answer by further polishing two satisfactory answers. Try to leave some time at the end of the examination to re-read your answers and correct any obvious errors. If the worst comes to the worst and you run short of time, don't just keep writing until you are forced to break off in mid-paragraph. It is far better to provide for the examiner a set of notes which indicate the overall direction of your argument.

Good luck — but if you prepare for the examination conscientiously and tackle the paper in a methodical manner, you won't need it!

Three dots (ellipsis) indicate where words or phrases have been cut from a quotation or where (as here) a quotation begins mid-sentence.

the curious idea of the crown as a place where Death keeps its court, and having once seized on this theme he teases out its possibilities in a series of fantastic images:

> . . . within the hollow crown
> That rounds the mortal temples of a king
> Keeps death his court; and there the antic sits,
> Scoffing his state and grinning at his pomp,
> Allowing him a breath, a little scene,
> To monarchize, be feared, and kill with looks,
> Infusing him with self and vain conceit,
> As if this flesh which walls about our life
> Were brass impregnable; and humoured thus,
> Comes at the last, and with a little pin
> Bores through his castle wall, and — farewell king!
>
> (III.2.160–170)

long verse quotation indented and introduced by a colon. No quotation marks are needed.

Richard creates a little verbal play-within-the-play, based on the medieval *danse macabre* in which personified death leads men and women a dance around, and finally into, their own graves. Death has already been shown at work in this play with the death of John of Gaunt, but Richard then seemed insensi- its reality. Now he is keenly conscious of its power to u human vanity and with a puny 'pin' reduce a mona esteem to nothingness. The splendour of his 'name', o elsewhere he expends so much verbal energy, is thus provided with a very different context, and he, at least momentarily, pierces through the façade of kingship to the common condition of mortality which lies beneath it. Indeed, Richard invites his hearers to 'throw away respect,/ Tradition, form, and ceremonious duty', and speaks of himself as a commoner sharing the same vulnerable humanity as themselves:

short verse quotation incorporated in the text of the essay within quotation marks. Line endings are indicated by a slash (/).

Line reference given directly after the quotation, in brackets.

> I live with bread, like you; feel want,
> Taste grief, need friends.
>
> (lines 175–176)

It is as if in the process of exploring his imaginative idea he anticipates the tragic lessons learnt by Lear and Gloucester in *King Lear*. It is obvious, of course, that he doesn't actually do so. For Richard this is merely word-spinning; he has not yet learnt what it really is to be reduced by bitter experience to the

book/play title in italics. In a handwritten or typed manuscript this would appear as underlining: <u>King Lear</u>.

135

We have divided the following information into two sections. Part A describes those rules which it is essential to master no matter what kind of essay you are writing (including examination answers). Part B sets out some of the more detailed conventions which govern the documentation of essays.

PART A: LAYOUT

Titles of texts

Titles of published books, plays (of any length), long poems, pamphlets and periodicals (including newspapers and magazines), works of classical literature, and films should be underlined: e.g. <u>David Copperfield</u> (novel), <u>Twelfth Night</u> (play), <u>Paradise Lost</u> (long poem), <u>Critical Quarterly</u> (periodical), Horace's <u>Ars Poetica</u> (Classical work), <u>Apocalypse Now</u> (film).

Notice how important it is to distinguish between titles and other names. <u>Hamlet</u> is the play; Hamlet the prince. <u>Wuthering Heights</u> is the novel; Wuthering Heights the house. Underlining is the equivalent in handwritten or typed manuscripts of printed italics. So what normally appears in this volume as *Othello* would be written as <u>Othello</u> in your essay.

Titles of articles, essays, short stories, short poems, songs, chapters of books, speeches, and newspaper articles are enclosed in quotation marks; e.g. 'The Flea' (short poem), 'The Prussian Officer' (short story), 'Middleton's Chess Strategies' (article), 'Thatcher Defects!' (newspaper headline).

Exceptions: Underlining titles or placing them within quotation marks does not apply to sacred writings (e.g. Bible, Koran, Old Testament, Gospels) or parts of a book (e.g. Preface, Introduction, Appendix).

It is generally incorrect to place quotation marks around a title of a published book which you have underlined. The exception is 'titles within titles': e.g. '<u>Vanity Fair</u>': A Critical Study (title of a book about *Vanity Fair*).

Quotations

Short verse quotations of a single line or part of a line should be incorporated within quotation marks as part of the running text of your essay. Quotations of two or three lines of verse are treated in the same way, with line endings indicated by a slash(/). For example:

1 In <u>Julius Caesar</u>, Antony says of Brutus, 'This was the noblest Roman of them all'.
2 The opening of Antony's famous funeral oration, 'Friends, Romans, Countrymen, lend me your ears;/ I come to bury Caesar not to praise him', is a carefully controlled piece of rhetoric.

Longer verse quotations of more than three lines should be indented from the main body of the text and introduced in most cases with a colon. Do not enclose indented quotations within quotation marks. For example:
It is worth pausing to consider the reasons Brutus gives to justify his decision to assassinate Caesar:

> It must be by his death; and for my part,
> I know no personal cause to spurn at him,
> But for the general. He would be crowned.
> How might that change his nature, there's the question.

At first glance his rationale may appear logical . . .

Prose quotations of less than three lines should be incorporated in the text of the essay, within quotation marks. Longer prose quotations should be indented and the quotation marks omitted. For example:

1 Before his downfall, Caesar rules with an iron hand. His political opponents, the Tribunes Marullus and Flavius, are 'put to silence' for the trivial offence of 'pulling scarfs off Caesar's image'.
2 It is interesting to note the rhetorical structure of Brutus's Forum speech:

> Romans, countrymen, and lovers, hear me for my cause, and be silent that you may hear. Believe me for my honour, and have respect to mine honour that you may believe. Censure me in your wisdom, and awake your senses, that you may the better judge.

Tenses: When you are relating the events that occur within a work of fiction or describing the author's technique, it is the convention to use the present tense. Even though Orwell published *Animal Farm* in 1945, the book *describes* the animals' seizure of Manor Farm. Similarly, Macbeth always *murders* Duncan, despite the passage of time.

PART B: DOCUMENTATION

When quoting from verse of more than twenty lines, provide line references: e.g. In 'Upon Appleton House' Marvell's mower moves 'With whistling scythe and elbow strong' (l.393).

Quotations from plays should be identified by act, scene and line references: e.g. Prospero, in Shakespeare's The Tempest, refers to Caliban as 'A devil, a born devil' (IV.1.188). (i.e. Act 4. Scene 1. Line 188).

Quotations from prose works should provide a chapter reference and, where appropriate, a page reference.

Bibliographies should list full details of all sources consulted. The way in which they are presented varies, but one standard format is as follows:

1 Books and articles are listed in alphabetical order by the author's last name. Initials are placed after the surname.
2 If you are referring to a chapter or article within a larger work, you list it by reference to the author of the article or chapter, not the editor (although the editor is also named in the reference).
3 Give (in parentheses) the place and date of publication, e.g. (London, 1962). These details can be found within the book itself. Here are some examples:

> Brockbank, J. P., 'Shakespeare's Histories, English and Roman', in Ricks, C. (ed.) English Drama to 1710 (Sphere History of Literature in the English Language) (London, 1971).
> Gurr, A., 'Richard III and the Democratic Process', Essays in Criticism 24 (1974), pp. 39–47.
> Spivack, B., Shakespeare and the Allegory of Evil (New York, 1958).

Footnotes: In general, try to avoid using footnotes and build your references into the body of the essay wherever possible. When you do use them give the full bibliographic reference to a work in the first instance and then use a short title: e.g. See K. Smidt, <u>Unconformities in Shakespeare's History Plays</u> (London, 1982), pp. 43–47 becomes Smidt (pp. 43–47) thereafter. Do not use terms such as 'ibid.' or 'op. cit.' unless you are absolutely sure of their meaning.

There is a principle behind all this seeming pedantry. The reader ought to be able to find and check your references and quotations as quickly and easily as possible. Give additional information, such as canto or volume number whenever you think it will assist your reader.

Texts

The New Penguin *Richard II* (Harmondsworth, 1969), edited by Stanley Wells, is fully annotated with a stimulating introduction. Andrew Gurr's edition for the New Cambridge series (Cambridge, 1984) also provides sensible annotation and an introductory essay which pays particularly attention to the stage history of the play.

General Studies (containing substantial discussions of *Richard II*)

Bullough, G, *Narrative and Dramatic Sources of Shakespeare*, vol. 3 (London, 1960)

Holderness, G, *Shakespeare's History* (Dublin, 1985)

Moseley, C W R D, *Shakespeare's History Plays: The Making of a King* (Penguin Critical Studies; Harmondsworth, 1988)

Ribner, I, *The English History Play in the Age of Shakespeare* (Princeton N.J., 1957)

Sanders, W, *The Dramatist and the Received Idea* (Cambridge, 1968)

Tillyard, E M W, *Shakespeare's History Plays* (London, 1944)

Wells, S (ed.), *The Cambridge Companion To Shakespeare* (Cambridge 1986)

Studies of *Richard II*

Hill, R F, 'Dramatic Technique and Interpretation in *Richard II*', in Brown, J R and Harris, B (eds), *Early Shakespeare* (Stratford-upon-Avon Studies 3; London, 1961)

Holderness, G, *Richard II* (Penguin Critical Studies; Harmondsworth, 1989)

Humphreys, A R, *'Richard II'*, in *Studies in English Literature 31* (London, 1967)

Rossiter, A P, *'Richard II'*, in *Angel With Horns* (London, 1961)

Longman Group UK Limited
*Longman House, Burnt Mill, Harlow, Essex, CM20 2 JE, England
and Associated Companies throughout the World.*

© Longman Group UK Limited 1989

First published 1989
ISBN 0 582 03792 1

*Set in 10/12pt Century Schoolbook, Linotron 202
Printed in Great Britain
by Bell and Bain Ltd., Glasgow*

Acknowledgement

The editors would like to thank Zachary Leader for his assistance with
the style sheet.